Tips for Success -
Running for Beginners

Carl-Jürgen Diem

Tips for Success -
Running for Beginners

Meyer & Meyer Sport

Original Title: Tipps für Laufanfänger
6. Auflage
Aachen: Meyer und Meyer, 2000
Translated by Anne Lammert

British Library Cataloguing in Publication Data
A catalogue record for this book is available from the British Library

Diem, Carl - Jürgen:
Running for Beginners/Carl-Jürgen Diem
Oxford: Meyer & Meyer Sport (UK) Ltd., 2001
ISBN 1-84126-072-X

© 2001 by Meyer & Meyer Sport (UK) Ltd.
Aachen, Adelaide, Auckland, Budapest, Graz, Johannesburg,
Miami, Olten (CH), Oxford, Singapore, Toronto
Member of the World

Sports Publishers' Association
www.w-s-p-a.org

Printed and bound in Germany
by: Burg Verlag Gastinger GmbH, Stolberg
ISBN 1-84126-072-X
E-Mail: verlag@meyer-meyer-sports.com
www.meyer-meyer-sports.com

List of Contents

5

Throughout this book, the pronouns he, she, him, her and so on are interchangeable and intended to be inclusive of both men and women. It is important in sport, as elsewhere, that men and women have equal status and opportunities.

About the Layout of this Book

The list of contents shows the structure of this book. The **chapters** and most of the sub-sections are **in themselves complete.** If you wish to read a particular chapter later then you may skip it and move on to the chapters following. This guide should offer you some orientation here.

The foreword looks at how this book came to being as well as its aims. Chapter 1 shows us that running has become the most important form of movement therapy today and indicates the positive effects of sensible endurance training on our fitness and health.

After this introduction you may choose to go on reading in the order that the author has chosen or decide to read the basics on energy provision (i.e. chapter 2) at a later stage. In this case move on to chapter 3. Here you can find tips for starting with endurance training i.e. advice about running partners and on clothing, weather, choice of route, running technique, training frequency etc. Instructions for correct breathing while running can be found in the next chapter (chapter 4).

As already mentioned the second chapter deals with the basic principles of energy provision while running. The author deliberately placed this chapter before those with the actual 'tips' as he feels that an understanding of these processes is an optimal prerequisite for efficient endurance training. These processes which occur during energy conversion are illustrated in simple terms and, for the sake of comprehension have been reduced to the bare minimum of processes in order to be as understandable as possible even for the 'medical amateurs'. Readers who are dealing with this theme for the very first time should read this chapter more than once.

In this chapter there are also descriptions of some technical devices available nowadays for the measurement of pulse and lactate as a means of monitoring training. With the aid of these devices it is possible today to seek advice on the right load 'dosage' even for beginners or in the area of mass sports. Readers should be aware of these possibilities. Whether or not a beginner wishes to purchase such training aids, and indeed which class and price category he goes for, depends on his personal goals.

Chapters 5 and 6 look at health aspects, injuries and overstrain. Chapter 7 offers advice as to the correct choice of running shoe. "Can one lose weight by running?" This question is answered in chapter 8 along with some advice on nutrition and diets.

The important theme of remedial gymnastics is dealt with in chapter 9 and special exercises for stretching and for strengthening the abdominal muscles can be found in the appendix.

Foreword

The daily cross-country run was a perfectly natural thing for my father. When I was a boy I sometimes accompanied him. Later on I still kept up these occasional runs but for a long time I had more fun with hockey, handball and volleyball. In the mid-sixties when mass races appeared I was shown just exactly what physical condition in endurance meant. At that time the fit 'grandads' i.e. the 50 and 60 year olds were streets ahead of me - in the meantime I had become a somewhat weighty 30 year old. This fact did not only prompt me to do running training regularly but is also the reason why I, too, belong to the fit grandads today!

In 1974 the DARMSTÄDTER LAUF-TREFF (a special Joggers' meeting/event) was founded by Heinrich Peters and Walter Schwebel. I was really enthusiastic about this idea because there I finally found training partners at the same level as myself. Up to then I nearly always had to train alone as most of my friends and colleagues gave up after the first go. Even my wife dared to go running with me once. After almost 2 kilometres she was completely out of breath and totally exhausted - a thing which was incomprehensible for me at the time.

The LAUF-TREFF idea of offering training to the whole family at the same time and the same place but taking account of the different performance capacities was very tempting for us. Up to that point one member of the family was out at sport every evening in the week.

My wife was brave enough to try it again, there was even a beginner's group in LAUF-TREFF. However this was a hopeless flop, too, as for some reason the group leader at the time started off with our steepest hill.

My wife's failure here became the foundation stone for this book. After becoming group leader and having experience in competition up to marathon level, I decided to take over the beginners' group myself. My motto was:

"When a beginner has enough courage to come to me then I as group leader must prove to him that he will succeed and that he was right to show this courage".

At the beginning it wasn't easy but I had people to help me. A great partner for discussions about putting theory into practice was Werner Wittesheim for example, who had a lot of experience with the cardiovascular side of things through his teaching sport for disabled. A word of thanks here to Dr. Johannes Arndt who was also much involved with the beginner groups for many years and who along with other group leaders of our LAUF-TREFF helped considerably in bringing my concept into reality.

A very special thank you goes out to my wife, as not only did she try again for the third time but from then on worked together with me trying out all ideas in practice. She also reached her personal goal - to be good enough for us to go running together without it being too fast for her and too slow for me.

I have been looking after the beginners in the DARMSTÄDTER LAUF-TREFF now for almost 20 years. This is a task which some people may see as a burden but for me it's a new feeling of success every time. The radiant eyes and the gratefulness of a person who is fully untrained - often overweight and short of breath, occasionally even disabled - who has managed to trot and walk in alternation for an hour, more than outweigh the loss of my own training sessions.

This book should show the beginner that it is more sensible and more successful when you begin with slow trotting and worthwhile (walking) breaks, instead of running the way we learned in school and the way it is often shown as an example in television.

Experienced runners can read a lot about energy provision in this book as well as advice on training optimisation.

At the same time I would like to address the group leaders of LAUF-TREFF in particular those looking after the beginners groups, as the right care of the beginners is the key to a good LAUF-TREFF's success.

Carl-Jürgen Diem

1 Running as a Form of Movement Therapy

1.1 How Did it Come about?

Why is cross-country running (jogging) so popular today? For years we only went anywhere by car, lift or school bus. Who ever went anywhere on foot? And movement is the very thing that we need - our organism is geared towards movement. Lack of movement leads to the diseases caused by civilization which we have today, cardiovascular problems and in particular high blood pressure, diabetes, intestinal problems to mention a few. These illnesses were almost completely unheard of after the war when there were no cars, little public transport, no overweight caused by too much food.

Did you know that cross-country running (jogging) was not an American but rather a German invention? The inventors were among others

Armchair
Beer
Cigarettes

➤ The great sports educationalist Carl Diem, who as early as 1907 organised a LAUF-TREFF with his friends on Friday evenings in Berlin's Grunewald; the slowest runner was the pacemaker.

➤ The doctor Dr. Ernst van Aaken, who was extremely successful with his use of running as movement therapy and who at the same time refuted the claim that long running was dangerous for women and children. Thanks to Dr. van Aaken it is now recognised worldwide that a woman's endurance performance capacity is excellent. He fought up until his death to prove that a child's endurance capacity is just as high.

➤ The entrepreneur Enzio Busche who noticed with several of his workers how endurance training improved their general performance capacity. As a result of this he called for the formation of LAUF-TREFFs. The German Sports Federation caught hold of this idea and today it represents a huge movement in motion in which most importantly the people are in motion too.

➤ Arthur Lambert, athletics coach and for years the driving force behind the "Interest Group of Veteran Long-distance Runners" who through his daily running was so healthy and vital that he could undergo a cancer operation at 90 years of age and take up his running again a few weeks later.

Emil Zatopek, a great idol as man and runner once came up with the perfect saying: "The bird flies, the fish swims; and man runs".

Next to walking, running is the easiest and most natural form of movement there is. Take a look at small children: they normally "run" and seldom "walk".

When I say **running** I don't mean the running or a kind of race that we normally get to see. Efficient endurance training for beginners and for mass sports should take place between 60 and 80% of the maximum possible speed. You'll be surprised how slow you find this speed to be. Accepting this running speed to be the right one seems to be the most difficult learning process for runners - well over half of them train at levels of too high intensity and thus inefficiently.

The easiest rough guide for finding the right running speed is:
As long as you are able to hold a conversation while running, you're training properly! If you're too out of breath to do this you're racing!

This difference between running (jogging) and racing is very important. The positive health effects of running on the cardiovascular and immune system are acknowledged today by all. In fact very slow running (trotting) is not only one of the first and most important rehabilitation measures after cardiac infarction but furthermore, sports-oriented doctors point out that 7 out of 8 infarctions can be avoided through proper endurance training.

In the chapters on energy provision and heart rate I will go into more detail on what happens in your body at the individual running speeds

and what possibilities we
have today for optimal
load control.

1.2 What Is Meant by Endurance Training?

The term 'endurance' can imply various different skills. One can show
endurance in front of the television or sitting in a pub. The ice-skater
needs endurance in order to complete his 5 minute voluntary exercises
as does the alpine downhill skier to be able to reach the finish after 2
minutes' sailing down the ski slope.

In specialist sports literature endurance is divided up into three time
periods. As this book deals with running, we should really define the
term **running endurance**. One must particularly pay attention to the
fact that endurance training is always a follow-up to a warm-up phase
(see chapter 2.7) which should be for at least 30 minutes. Only then
can one begin with endurance training - assuming that one is training
at a load level personally aimed for. The time periods are divided up
as follows:

1. Short-term endurance, i.e. endurance performances from 35
   seconds up to 2 minutes, e.g. 400 m and 800 m runs.
2. Medium-term endurance, i.e. endurance performances from 2 to
   10 minutes, e.g. 1 000 m to 3 000 m runs.
3. Long-term endurance, i.e. endurance performances over 10
   minutes. Specialist literature divides this category up further into
   endurance performances of >10 min, >35 min and >90 min.

The following chapter describes the positive effects of endurance
running training. The prerequisite here is that **training goes on for at
least 60 minutes,** consisting of a warm-up phase (30 min) and an
endurance training phase of 30 - 90 minutes in fat metabolism. A
training duration of one hour as is the practice in LAUF-TREFF for

example, provides an example of optimisation of the total time needed for changing, showering etc and the training effect.

This book is directed at all those who wish to improve their fitness and endurance capacity in the long-term endurance area as efficiently as possible, as well as experienced runners or LAUF-TREFF members who wish to find out more about the basics of training and/or would like to reorganise their previous training on a more efficient basis.

1.3 The Positive Effects of Running Training

Running training is the easiest and most effective form of endurance training. If you try to attain the same cardiovascular effect with another form of sport, e.g. with cycling, you would normally want to cycle twice the amount as there is less calorie consumption. This is because of the amount and intensity of the muscle functions necessary for this form of sport.

What exactly are the most important positive effects of running?

➤ Regular endurance training strengthens the heart muscle. The heart can thus perform more efficiently.

➤ The heart, being able to perform more efficiently, can pump more bloodinto the body with each heart beat, thus reducing the pulse rate. One could compare this with a small motor engine being replaced by a six-cylinder with higher performance.

➤ The resting pulse rate is lower. Then the pulse range between resting pulse rate and maximum pulse rate at top load levels widens. The heart becomes more elastic.

➤ The circulation of our heart muscle is also improved due to the growing or opening of the coronaries, i.e. the fine branchings of the arteries.

- We learn to breathe deeply into the tips of the lungs. In this way the oxygen conversion as the basic requirement for the oxygen supply in our blood is also improved.

- The ability of the blood to bind with oxygen (haemoglobin) as well as the release of oxygen in the muscle cell is put into training. This leads to a better, i.e. faster oxygen supply in the blood.

- Blood pressure, both too high and too low, is positively influenced. The tendency towards headache and dizziness is reduced as a result.

- Vein activity is improved. This helps to prevent the development of varicose veins.

- As well as strengthening the leg and back muscles regular running (at least twice a week) makes connective tissue firmer, whereby the dreaded cellulitis on the thighs or posterior is reduced or can disappear altogether.

- With regular running (at least twice a week) you bring your digestive system back into form , laxatives are no longer needed.

- Certain toxic substances, in particular heavy metals like lead for example, are emitted from the body mainly through sweating similar to in the sauna. However in the sauna you're putting your heart under strain, when running you're exercising your heart.

- Running means movement. Movement gives your metabolism a boost thus helping to combat many problems (headache, sleeping or intestinal problems, high cholesterol levels etc.) which can be attributed to the widespread general lack of movement these days.

- When you've got used to running in all weathers and you heed a few rules which will be listed individually later, spring and autumn colds are a thing of the past.

- Apart from the medical aspect there is an equally important psychological aspect - the relaxing effect. With physical activity, the warming of the muscles and the good oxygen supply to all body cells, in particular the brain cells, a relaxation process takes place due to the body producing ß-endophines which in turn bring on feelings of euphoria. Stress, anger, bad moods etc. are all worked off. No matter how angry I am, after an hour's cross-country run I am relaxed, peaceful and no longer take my bad mood out on my children or family.

► The most important thing however is the fun and the pleasure from one's personal performance ability. Many people take up running at the age of 40. Some of them haven't done much sport in their youth and in the last twenty years haven't done any sport at all. Many of these people suddenly discover a performance capacity which they had never thought possible before.

1.4 Medical Aspects to Be Considered

If running is so much fun and offers so many physical benefits why do we keep hearing and reading about doctors who point their finger, warning us? The proportion of medical doctors who recommend endurance training is still very small, as shown in a recent detailed study, but it is growing. The reservations they have are a direct result of our medical education and further education, in which far too little time and attention is devoted to the area of sports medicine and thus also to all areas connected with man's natural movement. Therefore query all bans on physical activity and running very critically. I mean - would you recommend forms of therapy which you're not familiar with yourself? Why should a doctor do so?

On the other hand some words of admonition are justified, e.g. in the case of acute illnesses or particularly from the point of view of orthopedic doctors, when they relate to our joints and feet and the ground on which we're running.

Many words of warning come from the USA. One mainly runs in the USA on hard surfaces e.g. cement and asphalt, whereas we have 70% more cross-country surfaces in Europe. In order to save our joints and to compensate for foot malformations (flat, splay and pes valgus) the runner needs a good running shoe. Unfortunately many of our runners neglect this really important item of *clothing* - and danger is lurking here (see chapter 7).

But with a sensible pace and the appropriate running shoe one can say YES, loud and clear, to running. In order for this **YES** to be one of the most pleasant benefits in this world even for you - without any side effects - the following tips and advice should help you. Your strongest opponent to combat is your weaker self - you must often try and outwit him in his bid to keep you from running!

2 Running Speed, Intensity and Energy Provision

Running is one of the easiest types of sport. The only equipment you require is a pair of suitable running shoes (see chapter 7) - provided you don't run barefoot - and appropriate clothing depending on the season.

In this chapter I would like to get you familiar with the most important reactions in your body. Looking at the different functions and the way they work together is not only exciting and highly interesting, it also enables us to put today's knowledge about efficient endurance training into practice in a relatively easy and comprehensible form. In connection with this I will also show you several technical aids available today for monitoring training.

I'm not talking about perfection or fanaticism. First and foremost endurance training must be fun. However in my opinion it should be carried out in a sensible and efficient manner. Day to day practice shows again and again that those who only rely on feeling, memories of school training or on the motto "A lot helps a lot" are training much too intensively and thus very inefficiently.

Let's begin with energy provision. We need energy to run. We gain energy through the intake of food. Carbohydrates and fats serve as energy bricks for the muscular system, proteins are for the building of cells and vitamins, mineral elements as well as enzymes are important helpers and fuels for the body.

Get to know about

➤ the regulation mechanisms in your body
➤ oxygen's duties
➤ the formation of lactic acid while running and what the amount has to say
➤ your resting pulse and maximal pulse and their connection to your training state
➤ how to find the right running speed for yourself through pulse measurement

2.1 The Muscle Cell

The muscle cell is supplied with carbohydrates, fatty acids, enzymes, oxygen etc. via the arterial blood in the arteries, waste substances which have formed e.g. H_2O, CO_2, lactic acid etc. are emitted via the blood in the veins.

Energy conversion takes place in the muscle cell..The number of existing 'muscle power stations' (mitochondrias) is important here for the conversion of energy. Endurance training can increase their number and thus improve the performance capacity of the heart muscle. The function of these power stations and what happens inside them is illustrated in the diagrams 2a-c. Diagram 1 shows a basic sketch of the most important elements of the muscle cell.

Diagram 1:
The basic workings of a muscle cell with muscle power stations (mitochondria) where energy is produced aerobically. In the muscle cell there are carbohydrate (glycogen) and fatty acids deposits. The number of mitochondrias, as well as the amount of deposits depends on the runner's state of training.

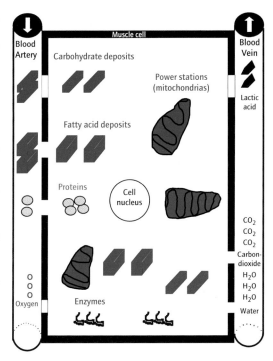

2.2 The Functions of Oxygen during Energy Conversion

The muscle gains its work energy i.e. the energy to contract, from the binding energy which is released when carbohydrate and fatty acid molecules are split. One can compare this process with the production of atomic energy - energy is released through the splitting of atoms.

We can do without the chemical formulas for the entire process of energy production as that is complicated. However the following points are important for further understanding.

➤ Binding energy is released with every splitting; the muscle can then convert this into a contraction.

➤ With every split comes one **hydrogen atom H**, which must be emitted out of the muscle cell.

➤ Waste removal is the responsibility of oxygen O, which combines with hydrogen to make H_2O. This combining is only possible within the muscle powerstations. The hydrogen is stored with a hydrogen carrier until an oxygen atom comes along and combines with it to form H_2O and take it away.

➤ The number of hydrogen carriers is limited. However it's vital that hydrogen carriers are there for certain splitting processes.

➤ In this way the current oxygen supply controls the ability to convert energy in each power station.

2.3 Energy Conversion

The muscle cell has three methods of converting energy. Whatever method the cell uses or is able to use depends on the current oxygen supply in each individual muscle power station (mitochondria) and on the energy reserves available. The runner cannot control the oxygen supply directly but can greatly influence it through the quality of the warm-up phase (see chapter 2.7), as well as through his running speed and/or his running intensity.

The first two methods of energy conversion occur through the splitting of a carbohydrate molecule which is possible without oxygen (diagram

2a) or with oxygen (diagram 2b). As well as this, the body has a limited amount of carbohydrate deposits (glycogen deposits) both within and outside the muscle cell. These deposits can be slightly increased through endurance training. If they are empty, then sport performances are no longer possible.

The third method (diagram 2c) occurs through the splitting of fatty acid molecules which must firstly be gained from fat. All bodies, even the very slim ones, have fat reserves in ample amount. Many people have too many fat reserves and this can be easily seen on the weighing scales. Losing these excess reserves is only possible through undernourishment e.g. fasting or through intensive fatty acid consumption e.g. regular endurance training. This means therefore that this process of converting fat into fatty acids can be trained.

2.4 The Three Methods of Energy Conversion

1. Through a single splitting of a carbohydrate **without** enough oxygen supply
   = **anaerobic** carbohydrate metabolism (diagram 2a)
2. Through the complete splitting of a carbohydrate **with** enough oxygen supply
   = **aerobic** carbohydrate metabolism (diagram 2b)
3. Through the complete splitting of fatty acids with **increased** oxygen supply
   = **aerobic** fat metabolism

This is the route the body must take when a muscle begins to work and the oxygen supplies are not sufficient. In this case the ring-formed carbohydrate molecule is split once into two parts, and the two oxygen atoms which form during this splitting process are stored with the two splitting products (pyruvic acid). Lactic acid is formed **(lactate)**. (A piece of advice : lactic acid has nothing to do with muscle soreness - see chapter 5.6!).

to
1.

The lactic acid is released out of the muscle cell into the venous blood circulation and makes the blood there sour. This hyperacidity of the blood triggers off an increase in breathing and heart activity via our central nervous system, in order to raise the oxygen supply in the working muscular system with a higher blood supply. (More details in the chapter 2.7).

As the carbohydrate molecule was only split once, only 5% of its binding energy could be used. The remaining 95% binding energy is left behind as lactic acid and is no longer available for the runner for the rest of the training session or competition. The lactic acid is transported via blood circulation to the liver where it's converted to carbohydrate within the next 24 hours.

This extremely uneconomical form is thus only suitable for short-term performances, e.g. sprints or changeover phase in the warm-up phase.

Still though, it's frightening how often one can see runners, in most cases training on their own but also even LAUF-TREFF members, who are led on by ambition or an incorrect perception of training beginning every training session at a level which is too high and then continuing at this level. They are not giving their body any chance at all to get out of this uneconomic and inefficient anaerobic training area in order to move into the aerobic carbohydrate or fat metabolism area. We call them *"the mad runners"* and many of the *"world champions in training"* belong to this group.

A simple comparison can make the process even clearer: Your carbohydrate molecule is a bar of chocolate with 19 sections which you take from your carbohydrate depot. If you dive into your bar without enough oxygen, you can only bite off one little section and have to pack what's left over with the remaining 18 sections into your rucksack. If you keep on like this you need for every new step a further bar of chocolate from your depot from which you can only bite off one square every time. In this way you're running down your depot to the power of 18 in a very short time - for a runner we're talking about 30 - 50 minutes. At the same time your rucksack is full of leftovers which are, as shown in diagram 2a, lactic acid. This means that you have done nothing but convert your entire store of carbohydrates into

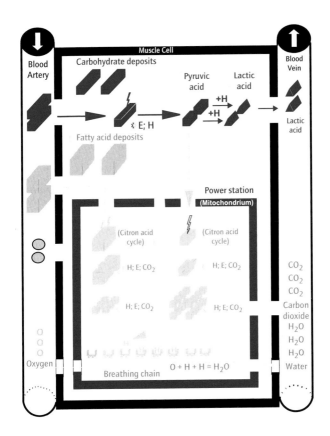

Diagram 2a:
A basic sketch of aerobic energy production through the single splitting of a carbohydrate molecule.

*Above: The first splitting of a carbohydrate molecule (glycogen) occurs after its activation ✔✔ outside the power station. Two molecules of pyruvic acid are formed. At the same time binding energy (**E**) and hydrogen (H_2) are released.*

Below: As all hydrogen carriers ⌊₀₀⌋ are busy at the moment the hydrogen atoms H_2 must be stored up with the pyruvic acid molecules. Lactic acid is formed (lactate) which flows to the veins.

lactic acid thus causing hyperacidity of your muscles. Now you need approx. 24 hours to reverse this state of affairs.

You might feel that you've exerted yourself and thus made a great contribution to your fitness condition. But you're wrong. You might have emptied all your deposits but you've only used up a small amount of energy. You've only converted the majority of carbohydrates into lactic acid and most of all you haven't worked off any fatty acids.

!

You have neither done endurance training nor fulfilled the requirements with fatty acid consumption for weight loss! (see chapter 8).

If on the other hand you are able to enjoy and relish one square after the other with the aid of oxygen, you'll get with the carbohydrates available 19 times further - in the optimal case - than through anaerobic energy conversion.

to 2.

The changeover from 1 to 2 is fluent and different from muscle power station to station. This phase is known as warm-up phase. Depending on load intensity and load increase one will manage to get to a completely aerobic energy provision from carbohydrates sooner or later: with the right approach speed after approx. 30 minutes (see chapter 2.7).

With a sufficient oxygen supply the splitting of the carbohydrate molecule outside the muscle power station will be continued inside. When all occurring hydrogen atoms are bound by the oxygen to form water and have been removed, one can reach an optimal energy consumption level of 95% i.e. to the power of 19 compared with the anaerobic carbohydrate metabolism. This is a significant prerequirement for all endurance performances.

As the training continues and the load exceeds the current oxygen supply then the energy provision automatically changes back over to the anaerobic form.

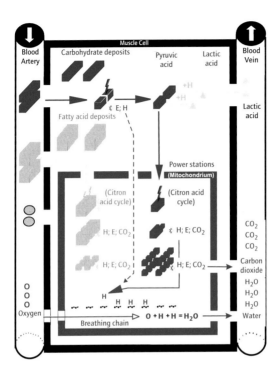

Diagram 2b:

*A basic sketch of **aerobic** production through the complete splitting of a carbohydrate molecule in the muscle power station (mitochondria). Centre right: If there are enough hydrogen carriers ⌐₀₀┘ free following the first splitting of the carbohydrate molecule then the pyruvic acid is transported to the power station where it is broken down completely in several stages. At each stage energy **(E)** is released. The existing hydrogen H_2 B turned into H_2O with oxygen, while the existing carbon **C** is bound to form CO_2.*

The changeover from 2 to 3 is just as fluent as 1 to 2. It is also different from power station to power station. The splitting of the fatty acids molecules is only possible within the muscle power stations. At the same time the **supply of oxygen must be approx. 15% higher** than for the aerobic carbohydrate metabolism as the fatty acids contain more hydrogen molecules than there are needed for binding. **The fat metabolism is actually the real endurance metabolism.** Whereas the amount of carbohydrate deposits in the body - as already mentioned above - is very limited and there is a minimal possibility of increasing this storage capacity, the body has on the other hand an almost unlimited amount of fat reserves.

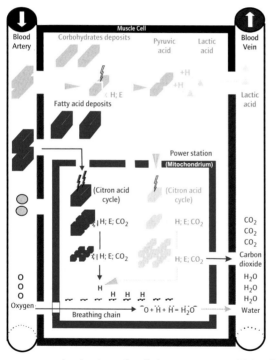

Diagram 2c:
Basic principles on energy production from fatty acids
Centre left: After being activated, the fatty acids can only be split within the muscle power station. This automatically requires free hydrogen carriers and a 15% higher oxygen supply, as the fatty acid molecules contain more hydrogen and carbon than carbohydrate molecules. At each splitting stage energy (E) is released. The existing hydrogen is bound with oxygen to form H_2O, the existing carbon C is bonded to form CO_2.

The conversion of fat to fatty acids is activated when in every training session possible the fatty acids **are completely used up**. The more regularly they are used up, the more often the formation of new fatty acids is activated. In this way fat is broken down and at the same time fatty acids deposits needed in the body are increased as the body always makes an effort to get further reserves.

Converting fat to fatty acids means to breaking down fat. The prerequisite for this is long (at least 60 minutes) but slow running.

If the load exceeds the current oxygen supply as the training continues then the energy provision automatically changes back to the aerobic or even anaerobic carbohydrate region. Whatever direction the energy conversion takes is controlled by the oxygen supply for the binding of hydrogen to form water.

2.5 Lactate Measurement Can Be of Help

You're going to say (and quite right too!) "I only want to do something to keep fit, what's this got to do with me?" However I still recommend you to read on. I'm neither a technology freak nor am I a person who believes that one can only carry out even the easiest of sports activities, e.g. running, when properly kitted out with the latest technical gadgets.

Drawing on my over 20 years' experience with beginners and trained runners I would like to show you in the next two sections how our heads, the weakest of all body parts when it comes to putting together efficient endurance training, can with the aid of simple technical devices be prevented from making easy but common mistakes in training. Furthermore I would like to encourage you to try out these technical aids when the opportunity arises. Lactate and pulse measurements enable you to determine your training state thus giving you a starting base for efficient training.

Lactate (lactic acid) is formed as described in detail above when muscle activity takes place without enough oxygen supply. Its formation is not welcome in endurance training or endurance performances. In the warm-up phase its formation is unavoidable and indeed vital. Therefore the rule is: **as much as is needed, as little as possible.**

Our goal in training is after all to be training in fat metabolism. Top performances in the endurance field, e.g. in a marathon or the Ironman triathlon, take place almost exclusively within fat metabolism.

The amount of lactate in the blood during or after a training unit gives us a clear insight into the type of metabolism we were training in, i.e. whether in anaerobic or aerobic carbohydrate metabolism or within fat metabolism.

The amount of lactate in the blood can be determined very easily with a drop of blood taken from the earlobe or fingertip. It used to be necessary to use laboratory equipment for a lactate analysis but nowadays it's possible with the use of a portable measuring instrument which the runner can carry along with him during training.

What's high, what's low?

Lactate rates are given in mmol/l. Rates between 0,5 mmol/l and 1,0 mmol/l apply for one's normal daily movements. In order to carry out training in fat metabolism the lactate rate must lie under 3 mmol/l. Neumann (Leipzig) goes so far as to recommend staying under the 2 mmol/l limit. The highest lactate rates with up to 25 mmol/l can be seen after 400 m and 800 m runs.

One differentiates as following for the area of running (diagram 3)

Lactate rate:	
<1,5 mmol/l	aerobic regeneration training
1,5 - 3,0 (4,0) mmol/l	aerobic endurance training
3,0 - 5,0 mmol/l	aerobic/anaerobic transition area (threshold)
>5,0 mmol/l	anaerobic interval training

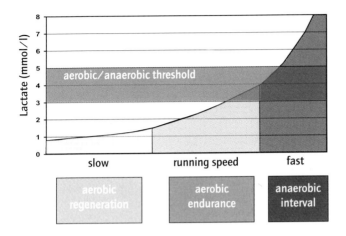

Diagram 3:
Lactate measuring instrument Accusport made by Hestia with a complete starter set

Sports literature often gives 4 mmol/l as the aerobic/anaerobic threshold. This threshold, however, is not identical for all runners, so it makes more sense to talk about a transition area.

The relationship between load (running speed) and lactate formation is not linear but exponential. Diagram 4 shows sample curves of two different endurance training states which were normed onto the forget lactate rate of 2 mmol/l (●). At the end of the training session (in LAUF-TREFF e.g. after one hour) at a given load (set speed) the runners should indicate a maximum of 2 mmol/l lactate.

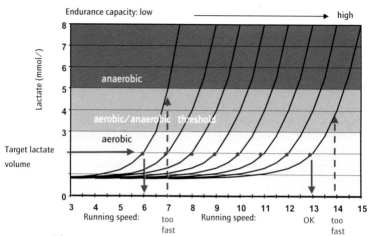

Diagram 4:
The relationship between load (running speed) and lactate formation is not linear but rather exponential. The sample curves for different endurance training states have been normed to the target lactate rate of 2 mmol/l (●), the maximum rate at a given set speed (see speeds above) which the runners should indicate after the training session (in LAUF-TREFF, e.g. 1 hour). The curves show simultaneously how the lactate rates rise or fall and/or which areas of energy provision the runner enters when he comes away from his planned speed and/or his optimal training intensity.

You can allocate yourself to the appropriate curve for your running speed. You can see from this curve what happens when, instead of the desired running speed (running speed at 2 mmol/l) you get faster or slower. For example if you run at 7 km/h instead of the requested 6 km/h your lactate rate rises from 2 mmol/l to 4,5 mmol/l thus already reaches the upper limit of the aerobic/anaerobic transition area. This means you're **not doing endurance training in fat metabolism,** but rather your energy is coming partly aerobic, partly anaerobic via carbohydrates. A runner who runs at 14 km/h instead of 13 km/h has a similar experience. Your individual lactate rate can be determined through regular lactate monitoring.

2.6 The Heart Rate

However, it would be too much of an effort to measure lactate levels with every change of load or speed. This is where pulse-taking helps us on as this is possible at all times without any bother. There are clear correlations between the pulse rate and the lactate rate.

The pulse rate (heartbeat) reacts to every change in load within a few seconds, whether load increases or reductions (see diagram 7). Contrary to lactate, the pulse rate is almost linear up to maximal load. There are two ways of allocating pulse rates to the different training areas:

1. One determines the lactate content at defined loads (= pulse rates) and can thus identify if one is training with fat metabolism or with aerobic/anaerobic carbohydrate metabolism.

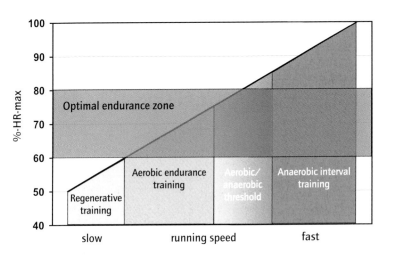

Diagram 5: Heart rates (as related to the maximal heart rate) for aerobic/anaerobic training areas

2. One sets the highest pulse rate at maximum load to be 100%. The rule then goes as follows:

Pulse rate < 60%: mainly fat metabolism

Pulse rate >60%: and <80%: partly fat metabolism, mainly aerobic carbohydrate metabolism

Pulse rate >80%: mainly up to exclusively anaerobic carbohydrate metabolism

The aerobic/anaerobic threshold lies within 75-85% of the maximum pulse.
If it's not possible to determine the individual maximal pulse rate with the help of lactate measurement or e.g. with the Conconi test, Hollmann offers a method for taking an adult's pulse rate which enables a rough estimate:

Maximal pulse i.e. 100% = 220 - age
Example: Age = 50 years: 220 - 50 = 170 (beats per minute)

80% corresponds to a pulse of 136 beats, 60% to 102 beats per minute.

This correlation between pulse rate and load depends furthermore on weather conditions, temperature in particular, but also the runner's state of health. Higher pulse rates are normal at hot temperatures which is why one should reduce one's load in such weather conditions. A higher pulse rate at normal temperatures is a warning signal from the body to cut down on load - even if the source is not evident. A check-up is necessary.

For these reasons pulse rates are taken today in all endurance sports as a means of monitoring training. They serve to help one train at an optimal level, i.e. efficiently. Taking one's pulse is therefore very sensible for beginners and in LAUF-TREFF as this is where people often train anaerobically at intensities that are much too high, i.e. very inefficiently. The belief that "(training) a lot helps a lot" is - if at all- only acceptable when measuring instruments are used as control.

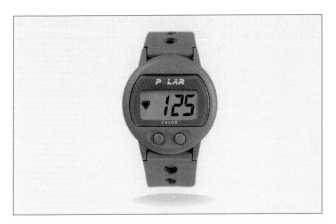

Diagram 6a: Pulse rate measuring instrument - consisting of transmitter and receiver, POLAR FITWATCH

Diagram 6b: Putting on the POLAR transmitter

Pulse measuring instruments are available from many companies these days. The most accurate ones are those with a chest sensor and a watch as receiver. The receivers are available in a variety of models which can be classified broadly into the following categories:

1. Standard watches with pulse display as well as adjustable upper and lower limits. They are suitable for runners who know their own personal training pulse areas and who wish to train within these limits or wish to go above or below these values.

2. Watches with interval memory capacity, target pulse values, average pulse rates and the information if and how long he was trained in the aerobic area etc. are required by ambitious runners who wish to monitor specific training loads with pulse measurement.

3. Watches with interval memory and a total memory capacity of 24 hours which can be evaluated on PC. Such models are of optimal assistance for coaches, training groups or runners who want exactinformation. With the computer evaluation it is possible to have the pulse sequence for a time period illustrated exactly in graphic and evaluated (see diagram 7 with data from a Polar Sport Tester). These are ideal for determining the basis and for monitoring purposes. With the help of the diagrams one can find out information at certain loads or set specific loads and check later on if they were heeded e.g.

- The level of load intensity (60, 80, 100%). Did you train at the planned level?

- Pulse under strain in the warm-up phase. Are you heeding the instructions for the warm-up phase (see diagram 7) - one of the most serious mistakes which many 'solo' runners as well as group leaders in LAUF-TREFF make.

- Load reactions to surface.

- Controlling load reduction phases (see diagram 8).

- Changes in training state.

- Recognition of health deficiencies, e.g. raised pulse rates, when the runner has a cold (also a cold that he hasn't quite shaken off yet), deficiency in mineral substances etc..

Running groups would need only one such device. Regular pulse measurements can be taken with the normal less sophisticated pulse watches.

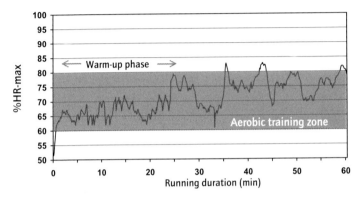

Diagram 7:
Pulse rate while running with constant load changes. The strong fluctuations show just how quickly pulse rate responds to a change in load. The warm-up phase with the lower pulse rates can be seen clearly which is about 20 minutes in this case. Each individual and also every leader of a LAUF-TREFF group can check immediately whether he had the right speed in the warm-up phase or if it was too fast.

There is a wide price margin for these instruments, at the time of printing prices ranged from about 50 Euro for the simple models and 230 Euro for the Polar S-series with computer evaluation (including interface and analysis software).

By keeping an eye on pulse limits according to Hollmann, the simple pulse measuring instruments enable you to control your training roughly or indeed more exactly if aware of your pulse-lactate correlation.

The examples in the diagrams 3 to 6 point out the various applications and evaluation possibilities. Many runners will be surprised how unusually slow efficient endurance training is.

2.7 Warm-up Run - the Correct Initial Speed

The correct initial speed plays a decisive role for both a succesful training session and a successful competition. Warm-up training differs according to the type of sport and takes between 20 and 60 minutes. Top-class marathon runners, e.g. twice Olympic champion Waldemar Cirpinski, take an hour for warm-up; for normal endurance training about 30 minutes are needed.

What kind of changes or adaptation processes take place in our body in these 30 minutes?

On a normal day our cardiovascular system works at an easy-going pace. Any increase in load must be signalled to this system. This occurs in various ways and these have not all been thoroughly researched. Apart from psychic influences and erotic stimuli, changes in metabolism probably play the main role here. For long - distance runners like us it's most likely the waste substances in our blood arising from energy conversion and in particular lactic acid, which are the relevant components for the activation of our breathing and pulse rate or the heart's blood pumping performance and the deep breathing.

Each increase in speed, be it the transition from walking to running or a speed surge while running, as well as a load increase brought about by a hill climb, implies a rise in energy demand of those muscles working already or of additional activated muscle groups. Every individual muscle cell has immediate energy reserves for this purpose for 6 - 8 seconds. This is about 10 - 20 strides for a runner at a slow speed.

This means that after 8 seconds at the latest the muscle cell changes over to anaerobic energy provision and, as described above in detail, forms corresponding amounts of lactic acid (lactate). In order to get through the aerobic carbohydrate metabolism as far as into the endurance fat metabolism you must give your body the chance to adapt as follows:

➤ The formation of lactate in the warm-up phase is both unavoidable and vital. Therefore the rule is: **as much as is needed, as little as possible.** This "as little as possible" can only be achieved through slow initial running. The pulse rates for this period should be under 70% of the maximum pulse and should be interrupted again and again by short load reductions - for beginners by short walking breaks of max. 20-30 seconds, for well-trained athletes by deliberate reductions in speed (see diagrams 7+8).

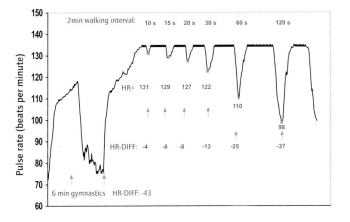

Diagram 8:

Load interruptions, e.g. due to 5 minutes' exercise or a walking interval of differing lenght (10 - 120 s), show just how much the pulse rate falls within this short period of time. In a training session and particularly in the warm-up phase such strong falls in pulse rate disturb cardiovascular adapation to the load as not only the pulse rate falls but the oxygen supply as well. - Compensatory exercises and stretching exercises are meant for the end of the training session.

The short load breaks (walking breaks) are there to vacate the hydrogen carriers in the muscle power stations thus creating an oxygen surplus enabling a changeover to aerobic energy provision. Extending the walking/load breaks to beyond 20 seconds is not physiological as can be seen in the example in diagram 8. The fall in pulse and with this the fall in oxygen supply is so drastic in breaks which continue for over 1 minute that they should be positively avoided. - Exercises belong at the end of the training session (see chapter 9).

The high occurrence of lactate in the leg muscles would explain the feeling that most runners have often experienced in the warm-up phase after about 10 -20 minutes, i.e. that your legs are made of lead and that **you're just not going to manage it today.** After 30 minutes this 'lead' feeling has disappeared and you can manage it after all. - The body is now warm, the oxygen supply complies with oxygen demand, and energy production takes place under aerobic conditions.

► In order to be able to supply the working muscles with sufficient oxygen, the blood flows in the body must be diverted towards the muscle areas with a higher oxygen demand. For a runner this means that the arteries and veins supplying the leg and foot areas must be made wide enough to allow the great amounts of blood to flow to there. At the same time the blood supply to the gastro-intestinal tract is cut off. - This is why one should not run with a full stomach as then the blood is needed for digestion. One can either digest or run. The adapation here depends on the individual training state.

► Pre-requirement for the complete energy conversion in the muscle is - as with a car engine - an optimal running temperature. This is at 38 -39°C. As can be seen in diagram 9, the temperature in the foot and calf area must be raised by approx. 10°C. This is only possible through the warmth created during energy conversion and not through outside factors. This is why we mention warming up/a warm-up running phase.

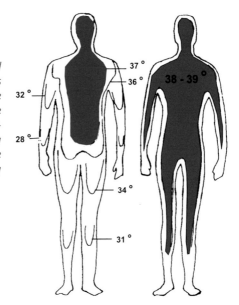

Diagram 9:
Left: normal temperature distribution
Right: For optimal energy conversion it is necessary to raise the temperature in the working muscles to 38-39°C. This warming occurs through the warmth created during energy provision.

2.8 Consequences for the Beginner

A beginner has only a small amount of energy reserves available, i.e. compared to a trained athlete he has a smaller store of carbohydrates and fatty acids in his muscles. For this reason he should not squander his reserves anaerobically, but rather look after them sparingly. In order to do this he must begin with slow trotting (60-70%) which stimulates his cardiovascular system, but after a couple of metres he must start taking short walking breaks for a maximum of 20 seconds (diagram 10). During these very short walking breaks the muscles' oxygen demand is automatically reduced to a walking level whereas the oxygen supply remains higher due to the higher pulse rate. In this way the muscle cells automatically change over to aerobic energy conversion. In these cases we're talking about a worthwhile break. This is how completely untrained beginners can successfully manage 1 hour trot-walk-trot wihout any danger of overstrain.

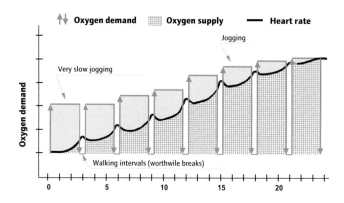

Diagram 10:
Load increase in the warm-up phase for the untrained beginner. Through slow load increases the oxygen supply is brought into line with oxygen demand. Furthermore, these breaks must be taken very early and must not be any longer than 20 seconds (worthwhile breaks).

Just how good this works in practice can be seen in diagram 11 of the pulse curve of a female runner in the beginner group of the DARMSTÄDTER LAUF-TREFF, where the group trots 5.5km in one hour and takes 20 very short (approx. 20seconds) walking breaks.

In 'antiquated' training guidebooks, which are still published today and even used in certain academic colleges for teacher training, breaks in the beginning phase are recommended to last for 1 - 5 min. As we saw in diagram 8 this is far too long. The pulse rate and oxygen supply to those muscles needed for running falls so dramatically that such training recommendations must be seen as completely unphysiological. They merely lead to premature tiredness as energy provision in aerobic metabolism is not being achieved. Do not be misled by such recommendations.

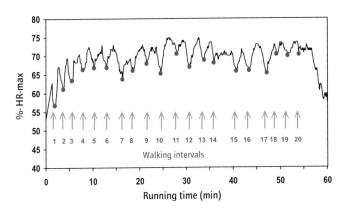

Diagram 11:
Pulse rate of a female runner in a beginners' group of the DARMSTÄDTER LAUF-TREFF with 5.5 km per hour. One can clearly see where the 20 walking breaks are taken in this optimally-led beginners' group. The quick fall in pulse rate also shows that the walking breaks may only be very short, i.e. no more than 20-30 seconds.

The secret behind the success here is to **take the breaks (walking breaks) as early as possible, in any case much earlier than you think you need them.** Diagram 12 shows where these 'worthwhile breaks' are for an hour's run with runners of different performance capacities. On a flat surface at a speed of approx. 7-7.5 km per hour one reaches a border area where it is possible to trot for an entire hour without a walking break.

Anyone who needs a walking (breathing) break on a flat surface when doing 8 km/h would be better to slow down a bit. If a person does happen to need a break because he just can't go any further then he's been going too fast. This break is no longer a 'worthwhile' break but rather a compulsory one: one can't go on any further because too much energy has already been used up and at the same time the corresponding amount of lactate has been formed. One must avoid this happening either through slower initial running and/or early walking breaks.

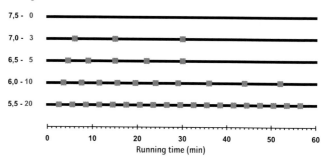

Running speed (km/h)
Walking intervals

Diagram 12:
Running (trotting) and break sequences for beginners and the less-trained runners for a 60-minute run. The early breaks are known as 'worthwhile breaks' and are the decisive factor for a run's success.

2.9 Consequences for the Trained Runner

The mechanisms involved with proper warming up are the same for all runners, regardless of whether you'd like to do a training run or a longer distance against the clock: e.g. 2 000 m or 3 000 m for a sports badge or the 15-30 minute running badge from LAUF-TREFF. Before you take on such a target, you must warm up with a run of at least 30 minutes with gradual load increases. Only then may you work on your target. The frequent excuse **"But then I'm already worn out!"** is unfounded as long as one increases the load at a suitably slow pace and 'worthwhile breaks' - either in the form of walking breaks or speed reduction - are included early enough (!).

Running the marathon distance within an optimal time is done with your head and not according to feeling. After a purposeful warm-up phase the important thing now is to stick exactly to the set time for the first ten kilometres and not be pulled along in a feeling of euphoria by other runners' higher speeds.

The quicker you get to the fatty acid metabolism over this distance the better your finishing time will be. High anaerobic phases in the first ten kilometres make you either run against "the wall" in the 35th kilometre or, you're in danger of being hit by "the man with the hammer".

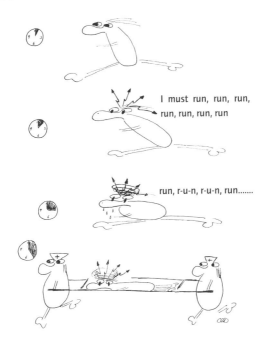

I must run, run, run, run, run, run, run

run, r-u-n, r-u-n, run.......

2.10 The Correct Running Speed

If there are no better possibilities available of controlling speed through pulse measurement, there is one good yardstick for finding the right speed in training, i.e. for running within the aerobic carbohydrate or fat metabolism:

Run at a speed at which you are able to hold a conversation with your partner!

!

This means at a maximum of 60 - 80% of your performance capacity. This is however not true for every metre. The conversation dwindles automatically with a conscious load increase. But the yardstick measure of being able to hold a conversation should be a clear indication for all group leaders and in particular for all husbands who go running with their wives. When the conversation dwindles in a group or the running partner gets more and more silent then these people are running within their performance limits. It's most often 'solo' runners who can be seen running too fast.

Finally a word to those who always want to train at their performance limits - world - class athletes who run marathon distance at 20km/h, run their endurance phases at approx. 15 km/ hour (=75 %) and their regenerative phases at approx. 10-12 km/h (=50 %). It's easier to understand this with a watch than with your head!.

3 The Beginning Is Always the Hardest Part

Running is one of the nicest and most relaxing hobbies around. Even here though it's true to say that the beginning is always the hardest part and by the time the beginner gets to see it more as relaxation than exertion it will have cost him a lot of sweat! But it's exactly this sweating that's important for us because firstly our skin pores are cleaned thoroughly and secondly - and this is even more important - many toxic substances are emitted from the body through sweating (e.g. lead, copper etc.).

3.1 The First Three Months

Despite all the enthusiasm and the best of resolutions it is particularly hard to get running regularly. Set yourself a target. Where running is concerned it has proved to be worthwhile to give oneself a time of at least three months with no excuses allowed. There are so many reasons why you're not going to manage it again today. For this reason try the following trick: enter the running days and times in your diary/ calendar and give these entries absolute priority.

Fight to the bitter end for every single jogging fixture! You'll soon see it's not that hard after all.

Don't get put off by the weather! You're going to be sweating anyway, what difference does it make if you get wet from outside too? Either way you'll have to take a shower. Don't wear too much when it's raining. You only need a nylon jacket where it's very windy - e.g. on open fields - but not in a forest sheltered from the wind. Anyone who has never gone running in the rain will be amazed how cheerful a soaking wet group of runners can be, and how peaceful a forest is, which in turn has a relaxing effect on one's body.

3.2 How Often Should I Go Running?

At the beginning the muscles react with a little muscle soreness as they do following all unaccustomed activities (see chapter on muscle soreness). Little aches and pains may also occur here and there. However don't feel uncertain or discouraged. You've set your target: to hold out for at least three months. By then most of you will be going running not for somebody else's sake but because you'll be fascinated yourself. Lay down exactly when you want to run, say on ...... - but how often in the week?

That's exactly it, how often?

Once a week is good!

But it takes a long time before any noticeable progress can be seen. The thing is - after three or four days our muscles begin to forget the training stimulus that we gave them by running. Therefore:

Twice a week is better!
Three times would be optimal!

More often though is not advisable for a beginner. After every load your muscles require a recovery or regeneration phase. How long this phase should be depends on how much and which kind of sport you did in your youth. Other factors such as how long you have not been active in sport, your current weight and state of health similarly play an important role here.

3.3 Choosing the Running Surface and Route

One can really run everywhere. Even in big cities there are - as we know from practice - ample side streets and parks where one can trot away if a person is only interested in keeping up his training target. The thought of this however for a beginner is more likely to act as a deterrent than encourage him to go running.

Ideal for running are flat forest and park paths layered or 'cushioned' with pine needles etc. Unfortunately though such a possibility is seldom available. We mostly have to make do with the normal field and forest paths. The quality of the surface and different gradients influence the running speed.

The beginner should avoid climbs if at all possible - which are determined to a large extent by the area - but in any case compensate for them through even slower *trotting* or *walking.* A hill-climb is a climb in load which inevitably leads to anaerobic energy conversion. On a gentle downward slope on the other hand you can quicken your pace somewhat, but only short-term. Steep downward slopes are not good for the beginner or the more experienced runner - they involve too much strain on the joints.

A flat, cushioned surface is the nicest one to run on. Very uneven paths demand more strength, make more work for the foot and knee joints and require the use of a very firm shoe with a lot of support and good foot guidance. For extreme cases or e.g. in the case of sand or snow it's advisable to wear an ankle-boot to save and support the joints (see chapter 7). For very soft surfaces e.g. soft sand or snow, one would need shoes with coarse treading and a lot of strength as it is difficult otherwise to get a good grip.

47

Rough, uneven paths and climbs present significantly more problems for women - particularly beginners - than for men. This is to do with women's smaller muscle mass and in particular with the quadriceps femoris muscle which is so necessary for running. For this reason it is important to demand a lot more in quality of a running surface for beginners than for experienced runners as in addition to the low muscle performance capacity beginners tend to have weight problems as well.

! **Generally speaking, the rule is: the lower the running capacity, the higher the quality of the track must be.**

.Asphalt as a running surface is better than its reputation in my opinion. Paths with asphalt normally have a very even top surface, in the summer months they often offer better shock absorbency than a dried out field or hard path. Because there is very little slippage in the push-off phase asphalt enables improved force transmission and thus a higher running speed. Those runners who 'drag' their feet somewhat during this process 'rub off' better than on forest and field paths. Cement, cobblestone and coarse gravel are surfaces to be avoided at all times.

A further advantage of forest paths in comparison to field paths: forest routes offer better shelter from wind and rain, as well as from intensive sun rays.

In Germany, for example, you are allowed to run on all forest routes admitted to the public. There may be exceptions however in the case of incubation and resting periods. If the contact is there, this is something which can be arranged with the forester. At this point I would like to pass on a request which has been conveyed to me so often by forest administrations: please only run on the forest paths and not just straight across the forest as this is where you disturb the privacy of the wildlife. On the other hand the wildlife soon gets used to people running on the paths - there is hardly any disturbance for the animals.

As well as the above-mentioned snow and ice, winter is often a problem for us due to the early darkness. It's particularly dark from mid-October to the beginning of December when the leaves are still hanging on the trees. Furthermore, fog hinders one's sense of orientation. With such weather conditions prevailing it is either possible to run through lit-up parks or, equipped with a torch, only on field and forest paths which are absolutely suitable .

Roads where cars drive on are dangerous enough during the day and must be avoided at all costs at night because of the high risk of accidents. Despite its monotonous nature the running track of a sports field is a better alternative.

3.4 How Long Should I Run for?

One hour has proved itself to be the ideal running duration. This is divided up into three phases:

1. 30 minutes' warm-up run at 50-max. 70 %
2. 25 minutes' load phase at 60-max. 80%, or alternatively with 2 mmol/l lactate
3. 5 minutes cool-down run (not a final spurt).

Naturally enough a beginner is not going to be able to manage to run for 60 minutes from the first training session onwards. So what's he capable of running? There is no general answer to this question. I've been looking after the beginner's group of the DARMSTÄDTER LAUF-TREFF for 18 years now, and there are always between 1 and 5 completely untrained runners in the group. Whereas we used to trot 200 - 500 m before we had our first walking break, nowadays I take this break after 100 - 200 m and if necessary even after 50 m. By constantly having about 20 short running phases and walking breaks in alternation we manage to trot approx. 5.5 km in an hour.

The 60-minute running training session is an optimization of the total time needed and of the success in training. Reputable authors, e.g. Hollmann, used to talk about only 10 - minute - cardiovascular activation daily. This was based on the the newly-gained knowledge of the 1960s and was correct provided it was preceded by warm-up training lasting 20 - 30 minutes. In the meantime Hollmann has extended these 10 minutes up to 30 - 40 minutes. It is still possible to come across literature stipulating this 10 - minute - cardiovascular activity, particulary in various running guide manuals. This is due to the fact that the authors of such guides have copied down these details without any query whatsoever and that they are not familiar with the latest findings. It's not really surprising when one considers that such theories are still being taught at academic colleges for teacher training.

3.5 When or how Soon am I Fit in Endurance Training?

There is no general rule or measure as to when a person can be considered to be *fit in endurance training*. I personally consider the *1 hour* to be a good yardstick, i.e. when one is able to trot for one hour without a break at 60 - 80% or with 2 mmol/l lactate then you're fit in endurance training. One reaches the lower level by running at a *speed* of about 7 km/hour.

There are many levels of fitness between the completely untrained person and someone who can trot at 7 km/h. Whatever level one wants to achieve is a question of setting oneself a personal target; whether or not this target is reached depends on how much time is taken up with training as well as one's individual basic speed. A detailed study on this topic was carried out in 1993 in the DARMSTÄDTER LAUF-TREFF and the result was that a third of as many as 400 in the groups run at 5.5 - 6 - 7 - 7.5 km/h; 70% of these are totally happy with this level and are not interested in improving their performance.

Similarly there is no general answer to the question: *"How soon can I increase my running speed?"* or *"How soon can I reach a specific running speed?"*, and this I can say after several decades of experience. Depending on inherited and acquired factors, some people reach their limit at 6 or 7 km/hour whereas others manage to increase their speed to 10 or 12 km/hour within a few weeks.

Obviously regular and long -term training will enable a runner to push his running speed limits up a little, however the 'basic speed' that one hasn't inherited is something that one unfortunately cannot acquire no matter how diligent one is in training. One can however work on improving endurance instead of being able to run one, two, three or four kilometres and this is something which one can achieve through training.

Making resolutions to be able to run for one hour without a break or to run a marathon after six months are in my opinion totally unrealistic. Such vows of success do more damage to the idea of endurance than anything else. A body which has not been in training for years must gradually get accustomed to the new loads in order to avoid overstrains of certain parts. Muscular adaptation takes 3 to 5 times longer than an improvement in the cardiovascular system. Doing less is often more effective!

3.6 Running Capacity and Weather Conditions

An individual's running capacity - and particularly that of a beginner as I have noticed - is influenced not only by one's general condition but just as strongly by the weather, i.e. temperature, humidity (sultriness), air pressure as well as oncoming changes in the weather. The fact is: there will always be good and bad days, one day you're springing through the forest like a young deer, another day your legs weigh a ton. This is when the group is a real help. By having a chat with your neighbour you don't notice your own problems as much, you can even surmount the difficulties because you're not thinking about them. As well as this, if you see other runners experiencing the same problems themselves then your own start to fade away.

3.7 Running and the Ozone Layer

Before anything else I would like to say that we have to do everything we can in order to reduce the amount of environmental pollution. This includes taking measures aimed at reducing the hole in the ozone layer in the stratosphere. However the many warning alarms and driving bans regarding the ozone layer in the past few years from certain groups are verging on hysteria and are in my opinion irresponsible. There is as yet not one proof from science or sport science that ozone values above 200 mg/m^3 are damaging to man. A study in Cologne showed that ozone values of 600 mg/m^3, i.e. three times as much as the warning alarms, brought about a decline in performance of 10%. There are even areas in the USA where values of 1000 mg/m^3 can be found every year without any known effects.

A study of the Ministry for the Environment in Hessen/Germany shows that there are contradictions between the different political statements. These contradictions can be explained by the fact that on the one hand the ozone in the city 'ozone centres' is formed under intensive UV radiation through car, household and industry fumes, and on the other hand is reduced again by the same fumes in the evening to starting values. In areas where the air is 'clean', equally high ozone levels are reached during the day but because there are no exhaust fumes they're still at this level in the evenings.

Is running possible when the ozone levels are high? The high ozone levels are not the problem - but rather the weather conditions which prevail at the same time. At temperatures above 30°C, combined with very dry and dusty air, the eyes and the lungs are irritated by grass and road dust. The combination of high temperatures and sultriness put a lot of strain on one's circulation.

Due to these simultaneously occurring weather conditions, it's advisable to plan the training units for the cooler morning or evening hours, or head straight for the swimming pool. One doesn't have to do without running training altogether, it's merely necessary to adapt loads according to the outside temperature and air humidity. From pulse takings you'll be surprised to see just how much of a cut down in speed is necessary.

3.8 What Should I Wear for a Cross-country Run?

You'll find it hard to believe: it's not what you're wearing **on the outside** that's important but rather **what's under it.** Wear either pure cotton underwear - for women down as far as the bra - or underwear made of microfibre. The more you sweat the important this fact is. Cotton absorbs sweat well, and you're less likely to have chafing at the underarms or - most importantly - around the nipples, a problem which affects both men and women equally.

Microfibres transmit sweat outward and the skin remains dry. Through this process there's less of that unpleasant cold sensation when one's clothes are soaked through from sweat. If you're wearing a few layers then they should match each other (from the functional point of view).

The important thing is to wear gear that is light and loose. Loose clothing prevents you from giving off too much warmth. T-shirts and sweatshirts should be made of cotton or microfibre. The good old cotton-mix tracksuit has had to make way for microfibre leggings or weatherproof jackets out of GORE-TEX and the likes. The tops should have a hood and zip at the front which one can open or close as one pleases. It must be possible to close at least one pocket so as not to lose the car or the house keys.

Nylon anoraks should only (!) be worn when there is a strong wind, particularly when you have to run across an open field, so as to prevent you from cooling out too much. Even when it's raining I find the normal training jacket better than the nylon anoraks as there's quite a build-up of heat under them! It is important to feel and keep warm but one should not end up sweating as if in a sauna - it doesn't help your running at all. You don't lose weight but waste a lot of strength. At the same time you lose more valuable salts than you should.

But how warm should I dress myself for running? You should always be a little more warmly dressed in training than in competition because the higher competition performance means that the body produces more warmth during energy conversion. In the summer or at temperatures above 20°C: shorts and a T-shirt or vest-top. Under 10°C: long trousers

and sweatshirts. When it gets to below freezing point it's not a crime to wear gloves, hat and long underwear. If the thermometer shows even colder temperatures, it may be a good idea to wear a scarf around the mouth for the first quarter of an hour so as to raise one's breathing temperature. After that the outer temperature is pre-warmed by the body to such an extent that it's warm enough for breathing.

If you're running **in the dark** - which is often particularly unavoidable during the winter - wear **snow-white** upper clothes in order to be recognisable early enough for runners coming toward you thus avoiding a head-on collision. Take this into consideration when buying your next jacket. Until then you can make do with a white vest over any dark-coloured pullover. Yellow or orange upper clothes are much weaker reflectors of light and do not fulfil this safety purpose in this light.

If you cannot avoid running on streets with car traffic please wear reflector strips on your arms, legs and back. Some runners also use indicators, which are suitable when you are running alone but which irritate other runners in a group. You should always take a little torch with you.

3.9 Can I Catch a Cold while Running?

As long as your body is kept warm through motion you cannot catch a cold while running. On the contrary - a large survey recently showed that through regular endurance training you get half the amount of colds as the immune system is given a significant boost with correctly carried out endurance training. It's only possible to come down with a cold afterwards, i.e. at that moment when you stop running and are still wearing damp or thoroughly soaked clothes.

For this reason:
Always change your clothes immediately (!!!) after training, if nothing else then the gear you had on on top - even when you have only sweated a little. This is the best way of preventing a cold particularly in winter!

Runners often just put a warm jacket, pullover or coat on over their running clothes. And who has not experienced that shivering sensation after 5 -10 minutes? Warmth is extracted from the body in order to dry the damp running clothes, and in this undercooling which automatically occurs in those parts of the body affected lurks the danger of catching a cold. Where there's a will there's a way dear ladies, be it in the form of a car or a secluded corner.

3.10 Who is the Ideal Running Partner?

Beware of your spouse particularly when this person is a good runner! Above all beware of husbands. They tend to completely overwork their poor wives who were willing to run in the first place. They seldom have sympathy with the argument that after years of not much physical exercise one can only trot very slowly at the beginning and is in need of many - and early at that - breathers (walking breaks). Many's the partner that has been turned off running completely because of having to overdo it at the beginning.

Diagram 13 shows what can happen when two partners with different capabilities train together and the better of the two sets the pace. For the better trained runner B this was run at approx. 80% which was confirmed by a lactate rate of 2.3 mmol/l. Runner A ran between 95 and 100%, i.e. at his absolute performance limit. His lactate rate of 5.6 mmol/l showed that he ran almost entirely within anaerobic carbohydrate metabolism which means this wasn't endurance training at all. The rise in the pulse difference between the two runners from 22 to 31 beats per minute shows the growing 'hyperacidity' and associated tiredness on runner A's part.

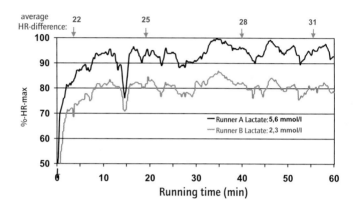

Diagram 13:
The pulse rate curves show what happen when two runners in differing training states run together whereby the runner with the better performance sets the speed. For runner B this was an optimal run with a lactate rate of 2.3 mmol/l, for runner A this was a fight within the anaerobic zone with 5.6 mmol/l. Further to this we can see the increasing 'hyperacidity' or tiredness on runner A's part. A's pulse difference climbs in comparison to B from 22 to 31 beats per minute in the training session.

Running with a group of runners who are just as strong as oneself - or at the beginning just as weak - is the easiest. Ideally, as it is indeed in many LAUF-TREFFs, the group is led by an experienced runner in such a way as to understand the major and minor aches and pains typical for the beginning phase and then get over them. A beginner who is looked after in this way will soon be an enthusiastic runner.

When a husband and wife have the same or almost the same state of training, regular running training together can have a very positive effect on one's marriage. As well as the relaxation effect and the common hobby there is the time that one has for running. When the stress has been worked off it is much easier to solve family difficulties.

3.11 Running with Children

Dr. van Aaken showed that children and youths are able to run long distances without any problem. To this day damages to one's health are unheard of. One can begin at the age of five or six. Children prefer running with their parents to running with special children's groups.

However they need to be talked to a lot when running. When parents and children do running training together it can be of great benefit for this relationship, provided, that is, that it is seen as a partnership, whereby the fun aspect of running has priority over training and performace pressures. If there's no talking it will become boring for children. They will prefer to stay at home.

Children (of normal weight) and youths have a huge advantage with their light weight, combined with a better strength/performance relationship compared with adults. There are no clear details as to the running speed but children between the age of 5 and 10 years can, after several days of training, run 5 to 10 km per hour according to their age.

A successful argument for convincing children how advisable and effective regular running training is, is the fact that running is the best foundation for many other forms of sport. It is particularly helpful for ball sports.

You cannot overstrain your children even on longer distances. When children can't manage anymore they simply do not move.

This is where the problem begins for parents or those in charge. The children can't go on any more! Parents who do not accept this but rather encourage or even force them to run further take the fun out of running for the children. For this reason don't put your children under pressure because it is only when they see running as fun that they will be successful on the long distances.

3.12 Running Technique

It is a widely held opinion that one should not try to correct one's running style. Sometimes it is said that one is not able to change it in the first place. And yet there are certain sequences of movement which must be heeded and - where necessary - have to be corrected.

Running upright:

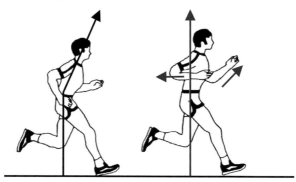

Diagram 14:
Upper body posture while running
Left: bent = wrong   *Right: upright = correct*

The lower arms should not go any lower than a horizontal position, as swinging down the lower arms too far counteracts the legs' lifting work. During the forward movement the lower arm should be raised up to an angle of approx. 45° as this supports the legs' lifting work to an optimal degree. The elbows should swing forward in front of the body in the process. Both positions can be achieved by training.

Raise your head or your chin. Many runners lean forward (Diagram 14). This means that the spinal column can no longer swing on the body's centre of gravity in a light or relaxed way - this in turn leads to intervertebral discs being under constant strain. When the upper body leans forward the back muscles have to permanently take on a support position at an angle that back muscles weren't designed for, causing tensing of the muscles and premature tiredness. As well as this, running with a tilted, forwardly leaning upper body hinders deep breathing.

Arm work rather than shoulder twisting:

The swinging movement of the legs has to be compensated for with a countermovement in the upper body. As the leg makes a practically linear movement the appropriate compensatory movement in the upper body should be linear too. Such a movement can only come from the arms - when the arms swing within the shoulder joints. As shown in diagram 15 the hands must be pointing towards the front just like the connecting rods of a locomotive.

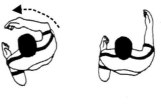

Diagram 15:
Correct arm movement while running: the arms are not to rotate in front of the body but should be held parallel to the body and pointing forward.

A famous coach once said: **"Running begins in the thumb and finishes in the feet"**. This means if you carry out the arm movement correctly then you'll move your legs correctly too. On the other hand, if you turn your shoulders and push your arms from side to side in front of you, it all becomes a torsional movement involving the whole body going down as far as your feet! It brings restlessness into the sequence of motion as well as causing tension in the back, shoulder and neck muscles not to mention premature tiredness. The torsional movement is a task, and it is a task which goes in the opposite direction to the one you're heading for.

Run upright and compensate the swinging leg movement with your arms; your arms then take over an important part of the running work!

4 Breathing

Running without panting?

"Running without panting!?" The German sports federation used this as their slogan in their initial running campaign. Unfortunately there was a lot of misunderstanding here - what was meant by this was running without getting totally out of breath and the slogan would not have been so  misleading if this had been clear from the start. *Panting, i.e. loud breathing,* is the most important thing for a runner.

4.1 Deep Breathing Can Be Heard

Many beginners believe that breathing aloud is a sign of weakness. On the contrary. Have a good look at top-level runners and notice how audible and deep, but at the same time how regular their breathing is both in competition and in training. If they didn't breathe so deeply they would not be able to achieve such high performances. As far as breathing is concerned you should follow the example of these top runners. Concentrate carefully on your breathing when you begin running. **Breathe out deeply so it can be heard!**

If you listen to yourself breathing out, you can monitor and test if you have really breathed out completely. Not only this - it is extraordinary just how calming it is to consciously control and listen to one's own breathing. You should make use of this calming effect particularly when you get *into difficulties,* e.g. at the beginning of a run or half-way through when the speed is too fast for you and you don't think you can hold out much longer. Consciously concentrating on deep breathing at moments like this often helps you over the hurdles. With time your body will start breathing again at an optimal level.

4.2 Breathe through Nose and Mouth

How can the beginner avoid getting out of breath? There are two ways: Either one reduces the running speed or one improves one's breathing technique. I don't need to say much about the first possibility as when we're out of breath our body automatically cuts down the speed. So let's work on the right breathing technique.

!

Correct breathing is the most important requirement for running

Our nostrils alone are not normally capable of bringing the necessary amounts of air into the lungs. This is illustrated with the following example: a beginner who is trotting at a speed of about 6 km/hour needs approx. 1 litre of oxygen per minute for this performance. There is almost 21 % oxygen in the air but the human body is only able to absorb 4 % of this oxygen. He breathes out the remaining 17 %. With high loads this can be even less than 4 % - this happens when one takes short flat breaths and pushes the air to and fro in the so-called dead space (the respiratory tract).

For the beginner this means that one must breathe in approx. 30 litres of air per minute in order to be able to absorb around 1 litre of oxygen. A person with little practice here will only manage to breathe in 0.5 - 1 litre of air through the nose with each breath and that's not enough. It would be like trying to blow up a balloon with your nose.

By breathing through your nose and mouth on the other hand even a beginner can manage to breathe in approx. 2 to 3 litres of air with every breath. In order to absorb 1 litre of oxygen even an untrained person would need only 10 to 20 breaths. Through regular endurance training such as running you can increase the oxygen supply in your blood, as the blood's ability to absorb oxygen is improved as well as its ability to transport.

4.3 Breathe out as Deeply as You Can!

The secret to good breathing is **exhaling**, as no matter how easy it sounds before you can breathe in you have to have breathed out beforehand. The average lung has a capacity of approx. 5 to 7 litres. Even with intensive exhaling about 1.5 litres of air are normally left in the lung and respiratory tract (so-called dead volumes). An effectivelung capacity is about 3.5 to 5.5 litres - according to the size of your lung. Running will not bring about a change in the size of your lung. However as already mentioned and as shown in diagram 16, an untrained person uses only a fraction - normally 2 to 3 litres - of his lung capacity.

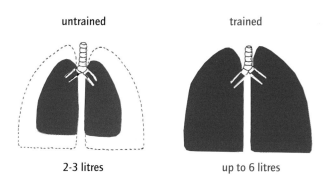

untrained	trained
2-3 litres	up to 6 litres

Diagram 16:
Active lung volumes
Left: untrained runner , 2-3 litres . . .Right: trained runner, up to 6 litres.

Reactivate your active lung capacity!

By merely breathing out consciously you can raise your *active* lung volume by 1/3. To do this you must exhale deeply and audibly - really getting the last air particles out - but without 'pressing'! In turn you can now breathe in more deeply. This is why you need only concentrate on deep exhalation when running.

4.4 Breathing in Sequence with Stride

There used to be very strict rules about this and even these days there's still a chance of finding several running books which deal with breathing and running rhythms in detail. When sticking to the one speed on a sports track or in flat areas these rhythms are regulated automatically. But you can forget all the theories available when you head into hilly territory. There are no set rules any more for going up and down hills. Your personal form and the weather conditions on that particular day also play a role. On days when we have trouble running we have to breathe more - either more deeply or more often. Sticking to fixed rules is more of a disadvantage than anything else because with a beginner in particular the breathing-stride relationship is permanently changing with the ever improving running and breathing techniques. Breathe as often as you feel is necessary and don't narrow yourself down to useless rules.

4.5 Abdominal or Diaphragm Breathing instead of Chest Breathing

Chest breathing is too flat and the soldiers' saying *"chest out stomach in"* may look smart, but it only restricts one's breathing. What's the easiest way of testing whether or not one is breathing correctly?

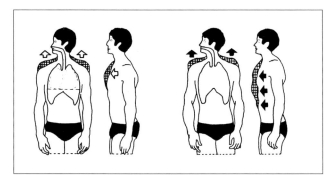

Diagram 17: Breathing:
Left: incorrect = chest breathing only   Right: correct = chest and abdominal breathing

Lie on your back, when breathing in, your chest and more importantly your stomach must swell upward or outward (Diagram 17). They sink back down again when you're breathing out. In order to test if you're doing this correctly and not 'pressing' place your hands to the side of your ribs. When breathing in you should feel your ribs opening up and therefore the stretching of the thorax.

4.6 Do I Breathe through the Mouth even in Cold Weather?

Opinions differ on this matter. Those from the medical field have as yet not been much help to us either as they are normally busy looking at sick people. Unfortunately they are seldom seen anywhere near experienced long-distance runners. There have been several scientific experiments but the results are not able to be generalised as yet.

Therefore let me tell you myself and my colleagues have learnt over the years:

I've never had any problems even when the temperature was - 20°C. By the time the cold air got to my lungs it had already been warmed up enough in my opinion. I have never caught a cold from running - but rather on the odd occasion after a run when I decided to have a *chat* first before changing into dry things.

Extra care must be taken however on very windy days and particularly when you have to run across an open field. In weather conditions like this you should prevent yourself from cooling out too much by wearing a nylon jacket, as the intake of cold air is only pleasant as long your body is warm and 'steaming'.

For those who are very sensitive, a scarf can be of help on extremely cold days.

4.7 Stitches in the Side

A *stitch* in one's side is caused by many different things. The actual cause itself is still not known. Three theories are under discussion at the moment:

1. When the stomach is too full or filled with food that has not been digested enough stitches to the left of the stomach are the result.

2. Capsule tension in the spleen and/or liver due to the high back flow of blood from the leg - pelvis area leads to pain on the right hand side.

3. A poor supply of oxygen to the diaphragm can cause stitches on both sides.

We can also categorise the stitches according to when they occur:

➤ The first type of stitch occurs shortly after starting to run, i.e. after 5 - 15 minutes. The high blood circulation in the body or a poor supply of oxygen to the diaphragm at this moment is supposed to be the cause here. This type of stitch occurs mostly in the first few weeks of training - a well-trained runner hardly gets it at all.

One can combat this stitch by reducing one's running speed (and similarly one's oxygen demand) or alternatively by consciously breathing (out) - this will get rid of it most of the time. The stitch will be gone after a few minutes. But if not, then definitely after 20-25 minutes when the body is warmed up and oxygen demand has dropped in the process.

➤ The second type of stitch appears mostly after at least 40 minutes and is caused in most cases by problems with digestion, e.g. flatulence. This affects runners - particularly female - with a slow digestive system who have either spent the day sitting down or who have eaten food which is hard to digest or simply too much food. Running stimulates bowel movement and there is possibly a build-up of wind in the process. Dr. van Aaken - one of the great founders of endurance training - hit the nail on the head (albeit somewhat profanely) when he characterised the problem as *"a fart that can't get out"*. And this is the very thing that you have to do - let it out! *How* is up to you - some solve the problem by strongly 'kneading' the stomach which helps let the air out whereas others have to jump in behind a bush. Be comforted by the fact that regular running causes such a improvement in your digestive system that after a short time you won't have these problems any more. On the contrary, if you had been relying on laxatives up to this you will soon be able to do without. One can combat this type of stitch by not eating anything which is hard to digest before your run or by emptying the bowels as much as possible beforehand.

➤ The third type of stitch is normally peculiar to competitive runners. We often see it ourselves with world-class athletes when they have problems with the competition speed or with marathon runners from the area of mass sports when they reach a phase of total exhaustion after running for 3 to 4 hours. The pulse rate climbs in this phase without there being a load increase (fatigue pulse), the energy reserves are empty and the majority of muscles are overacidified. The only preventative measure in this case is the right dosage of speed during competition, the only way to combat it is by drastically reducing speed.

4.8 Adaptation Problems for the Untrained Beginner

Stitches in the side are not the only thing affecting beginners. Compared with the more experienced runners they have a series of adaptation problems which all add up to become a considerably higher cardiovascular load:

➤ An untrained muscle needs more oxygen than a trained one for the same performance.
➤ An untrained muscle needs twice as much time as a trained one to adapt to a higher load.
➤ The release of oxygen in the muscle powerstations is a much slower process for the untrained runner, i.e. per unit of time he has less oxygen available for binding with hydrogen than the trained runner.

➤ An untrained person has less blood and has thus fewer red cells available for transporting oxygen.

➤ An untrained person has fewer muscle power stations and thus fewer places available for the short-term storage of hydrogen atoms or for their binding with oxygen.

➤ Due to the untrained runner's flat breathing - a beginner does not breathe out far enough and so breathes in 'flatly' - only part of his lung capacity is used for oxygen exchange.

➤ The untrained runner has a greater proportion of waste substances. Because there is less blood flow in general the body gets to be 'purified' much more seldom.

All these problems are enhanced by the fact that within the first 30 minutes, i.e. before the body (muscular system) has reached its working temperature - just like a car engine - more oxygen (fuel) is needed because of the greater amount of anaerobic energy conversion than when the body is warmed up.

So what can the beginner do about this? He must reduce his oxygen demand by easing the load with slower running or with walking or by raising his oxygen supply with better breathing. Or he can do both.
You know now : better breathing means consciously concentrating on breathing out further.

5 Is a Visit to the Doctor Necessary before Taking up Running?

When the German sports federation brought the LAUF-TREFF movement to life in 1974 all people over 40 years of age were recommended to consult their doctor before taking up running. Some people from the medical field still occasionally insist on this. However luckily enough this general recommendation has not proved necessary in practice. Furthermore, such a recommendation is only rational when very thorough examinations from the sports medicine area are carried out, and even then there is no guarantee that potential dangers to one's health will be recognised.

Where justified however, e.g. in the case of very high blood pressure, diabetes or acute problems, it would be advisable to see a doctor - and if possible one who has a positive attitude to sport. An orthopedic doctor may be the right person. - In some cases and under certain conditions cycling or swimming may be a more suitable form of movement/endurance training due to the lesser amount of strain on the joints.

You should never run with a feverish cold, 'flu or a stomach bug! When the infection has passed over it's a good idea to wait another two or three days and then begin again with a *light* form of training.

5.1 Difficulties while Running or Due to Running

Whether it's a long walk, a cycle, or a long time spent bending, e.g. picking strawberries, our body reacts to every unaccustomed physical activity and sends the odd signal or two. This shows us that this activity does not fit in with our current state of training.

When starting with continuous running there is a series of typical signals, e.g. from muscle soreness in the calves or thighs, pains in the foot or the knee, stitches in one side, strong palpitations up to bad sleep. These beginners' problems ought to gradually fizzle out with every further session of training at a running speed determined by one's performance capacity.

A visit to the doctor (best would be a doctor who goes running himself or who at least has a positive view of sport) is always advisable when the pain is constant, but beware of doctors who want to give you an injection immediately - a better cure is often exercise without load/strain.

5.2 Strong Palpitations or Insomnia

Strong palpitations and insomnia are nearly always a sign that the load while running was too high for you. The first thing you must do here is take a look at your running speed and particularly your starting speed in the first 20 - 30 minutes.

5.3 Blisters

Blisters are either the result of badly fitting shoes or unsuitable socks. Shoes often fit badly because they are tied badly. Therefore check that you have tied your shoes carefully and tightly enough.

It is possible to adjust a shoe's fitting by either changing the socks you wear (thick - thin) or by changing the insoles - this is normally an easy thing to do. Insoles are available in a variety of forms and thicknesses for filling the shoe better thus preventing you from slipping inside your shoe.

5.4 Injuries

Running is a form of sport with few injuries. All the same you're never immune to scrapes and grazes as a result of a fall or injuries like twisting one's ankle etc. Normally even accidents like these are of little consequence. But it is through these very grazes which may only be bleeding slightly that you can encounter *tetanus*. You should always be vaccinated against tetanus because you never know when you might graze your skin. A tetanus infection is not only extremely painful but it's also mostly fatal.

When your ankle gives way from underneath you the result is normally a painful overstrain of the outer ankle joint ligaments. Cold compresses are enough when it is a simple strain. However even if you prefer treating symptoms yourself it is wise to go the (orthopedic) doctor the next day if it is still swollen and painful.

You can also end up having a partial or complete tearing of the ligaments at the bone. The slightest suspect of this and you definitely must consult a doctor as a proper diagnosis can only be achieved with an X-ray.

5.5 Hardening of the Calve Muscles

Hardening in the calves, often described as being like muscle soreness, is often the result of your foot having not enough support in your shoe (your foot is *gliding* in the shoe) which in turn leads to an overstrain of the calf muscles. Changing over to (buying) a more suitable running shoe nearly always guarantees immediate success.

A further cause of this can be your running style if you only run on the tips of your toes or the balls of your feet. As a beginner you are not used to putting the weight on the front of your foot and this can similarly lead to tensing of the calf muscles. If you set down on your heel and then let your entire foot 'unroll' this tensing will stop.

5.6 Muscle Soreness

As we know today muscle soreness has absolutely nothing to do with the formation of lactic acid during energy conversion.

Muscle soreness which everyone has experienced at some time or other, normally occurs after any physical activity new to the body causing a painful restriction in movement of the overworked muscles in question.

An overstraining of the muscles occurs during their so-called passive load phases. Let me illustrate this with an example. When you run uphill you must use your leg muscles to help in actively gaining the strength or force needed to lift your body weight. As your body senses, and in particular your eyes, also perceive that a lot of muscle work is needed here, you automatically tense up enough muscles so as to be able to lift up your body.

The exact opposite occurs however when running downhill. If your body senses are not trained enough they will perceive that running slightly downhill is *easy* and therefore no strength is required. If this is the case, not enough muscles will be tensed up in preparation. The result is that far too few muscles have to take the weight of your body.

At the very least you can end up tearing the small so-called Z-discs of the inner muscle. The breakdown and build-up again takes 3-4 days. Unlike a tearing of the muscle fibre or of the muscle itself, muscle soreness leaves no scars or weaknesses but rather we assume today that the muscle is intensified in this particular area through the formation of additional mini-fibres.

One can prevent muscle soreness to a certain extent by warming up thoroughly and pre-stretching the muscles as well as through slow and appropriate load increases. The body has to learn how to co-ordinate perception and muscle effort.

The rule is for the treatment of muscle soreness: movement but no strain. Every movement enhances blood flow thus speeding up the healing process. Massages and further strain, e.g. running on further or gymnastics, are strictly forbidden.

6 What Every Runner Should Know about his Joints

Very many runners, male and female, start becoming actively involved in sport at a good age, either for the very first time or after a break of 10 or 20 years. As well as the normal muscle soreness, pains in the joints or the muscles can occur after a while. For distance runners these problems typically occur in the foot, knee and hip joints or in the calf and thigh muscles. However the root of the problem is normally to be found in our feet. Only one out of every three persons has 'perfect' feet these days. The rest of us have more or less pronounced fallen arches, flat feet, splay feet or pes valgus and sometimes even combined.

How well do you know your feet?

But what have these malformations of our feet to do with pains in our knees, our thighs, or even our hips or our back? A lot, I can tell you!

To aid comprehension here is a simple explanation of our anatomy:

Our joints are held together by ligaments and moved by muscles. The muscles always end in tendons. These have the task of attaching the muscle ends to the bone or connecting several muscles together. For a joint to be put into motion it is necessary for the muscle-tendon combinations to cover at least one, but often two or three joints. This is the case both for many thigh muscles as well as for calf muscles. The former go from the pelvis or the hip along the hip joint, the thigh, the knee joint and are then attached to the shin- or the calf-bone. It's similar with the calf muscles. One part begins below the thigh and down below they are then attached to the bones of the feet by the Achilles tendon, i.e. they cover the knee and ankle joints.

This combination of tendons and muscles is one unit and the rule is the same as for mechanics: they are only as strong as their weakest part. Deformed feet, depending on how serious they are, lead to a faulty loading of the muscles, tendons and joints. The pain that occurs is a sign of overload/overstrain of a particular part of the body, i.e. the *'weakest'* part.

The pain can hit your foot, the Achilles tendon, your knee or your thigh but in nearly all cases the root of the problem - provided that it does come from running - is in the foot-shoe combination!

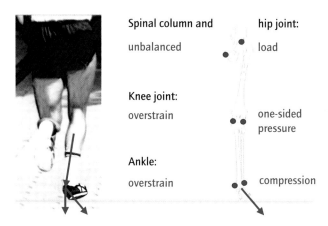

Spinal column and   hip joint:

unbalanced   load

Knee joint:
overstrain   one-sided
pressure

Ankle:
overstrain   compression

Diagram 18:
Effect of a marked pes valgus on the joints

These pains can also affect runners who have been running for a number of years when they suddenly raise training frequency or training duration.

As we are unable to screw off our feet and replace them with new ones we have to compensate for their shortcomings with the correct shoe. For this reason the shoe is the most important *item of clothing* there is for a runner! All the others are totally second-rate. But it's amazing how many runners you see wearing sports hall shoes, tennis shoes or even cheap shoes from the bargain-corner in a department store! In many cases the mere changeover to a good running shoe with a good inner sole for both the foot and the heel has corrected the problem thus alleviating the pain caused by the overstrain.

6.1 Knee Problems

Knee problems occur repeatedly when one takes up running and can be seen as harmless when they disappear again after five or six runs.

If they don't go away or if they only appear after a long period of training then this is an almost certain sign that you're wearing a faulty or unsuitable (for you) running shoe, and/or you have deformed feet which require the use of special insoles as is particularly the case with pes valgus (see diagram 18). An examination by an orthopedic doctor is necessary here.

6.2 The Achilles Tendon

According to my observations, long distance runners, who touch down with the heel 95% of the time, have significantly fewer problems with their Achilles tendon than those who touch down with the front of their foot. The front-foot runners are mainly former middle-distance runners who haven't moved away from their usual style of running. They touch down around the ball of the foot and then bounce to the ground with the heel. In the process the Achilles tendon is severely, i.e. very quickly, stretched and is under approx. 50 % more strain than in the case of runners who touch down with the back of the foot.

The most logical cure here is a change in running technique, i.e. towards a touch - down with the back of the foot. Putting this piece of advice into practice doesn't seem to be that easy as I have often seen. The head must win the battle here against one's own feeling - some are helped by the pain caused by recurring inflammation of this Achilles tendon.

6.3 Foot Malformations and their Consequences

Foot malformations are not there from birth but rather acquired. 99% of all babies are born with optimally developed feet. For their further development the babies' feet need an optimally developed support system from the trunk. However very few babies or toddlers manage to acquire this as most of them are put sitting down too early (passively) or are carried incorrectly. The foundation stones for later deformities have been laid.

As well as this, later on in life we not only neglect to look after our feet, e.g. by training them with foot exercises, we also punish them even more with unsuitable shoes or shoes that are too small (1 to 2 sizes with every second child!).

For all problems with muscles, tendons and joints from the foot to the knee, the pelvis, the spinal column up as far as the head you should first of all have your feet examined for malformations (fallen arches, splay foot, pes valgus, hollow foot). Find out if your legs are the same length.

It is possible to measure differences in leg length; differences of more than 1 cm can be partly compensated for.

Fallen arches, splay and hollow feet can be identified through footprints. Fallen arches even in the extreme form (flat feet) seldom present problems when running. Pes valgus can be supported with an appropriate insole. However there are hardly any corrective remedies for hollow feet.

Apart from splay feet, pes valgus is the main cause of pain in the joints particularly in the knees. It should be analysed in three phases: firstly in static position, i.e. when standing, and in movement twice, i.e. while running. Running should be carried out both barefoot and with a running shoe.

These two tests are decisive for the diagnosis of the level of overstrain as worn-out or unsuitable running shoes can significantly enhance the pes valgus components thus trigger off overstrain of individual joints.

In order to make a dynamic analysis a treadmill and a video camera with a switch for individual shots of a specific area is needed. Best would be a camera with built-in angle analysis. Unfortunately there are very few doctors with such equipment. On the other hand however a number of orthopedic shoemakers and certain sports stores who offer particularly good advice on running shoes are equipped to make such diagnoses. As you yourself are able to see this intensification of your foot deformities in slow motion on video film, it is not a question of a doctor's competence when he prescribes a better fitting running shoe but a question of taking these precautionary health measures.

7 The Right Running Shoe - Our Most Important Item of Clothing

Why is the shoe so important?

► **The shoe is the connection between your foot and the ground! Unlike all other items of clothing it exerts mechanic stress on your body which unfortunately can lead very quickly to faulty loads.**

To this day unfortunately the importance of a shoe's task is still widely ignored - even by orthopedic doctors. The majority of pains in the joints or the muscles can be attributed to an unsuitable or a worn-out shoe as well as a shoe- heel gone crooked. The best medical treatment of an overstrained part of the body won't be a long-term success if you don't attack the cause of it in the first place. But what doctor automatically wants to have a look at joggers' running shoes when they come to him with muscle and joint problems? In some cases the diagnosis is not *"Arthrosis"* but rather: *"Go and buy yourself new running shoes immediately!"*

From our standpoint today a perfect training shoe is the most important requirement for running training to be not only good for our cardiovascular system but for our joints too. The harder the surface is that you run on, the more important it is that you choose the right training shoe otherwise your foot deformities will be even more pronounced.

There is **no one good shoe** which is equally suitable for all runners. A particular model can be ideal for one runner's running requirements and be a catastrophe for the next runner. Certain other specific factors (when, where, how often, running conditions) play a decisive role for the individual runner. For this reason it is completely nonsense for shoes to be evaluated as *'good'* or *'unsatisfactory'* (even when certain reputable establishments for testing market goods do so it is still nonsense!) or be awarded points or whatever.

Choosing a really suitable running shoe is very difficult for all runners especially for a beginner and particularly difficult when he's a good bit overweight. There are over 300 different models of running shoes on sports store shelves, in the sports departments of large chain stores or in shoe stores; in addition to this, there are new 'cheap' models and imitations of well-established models available every day.

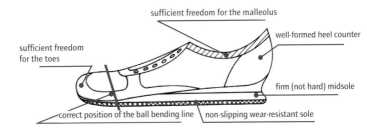

Diagram 19:
The most important parts of a shoe

A running shoe must

➤ **fit you perfectly** from the beginning. Your heel must be **firmly in place,** it mustn't slip. Your toes must have **enough room to move.** Due to the better blood flow your foot gets larger from running compared with walking. When buying running shoes don't automatically assume that they will be the same size as your normal everyday shoes. Sizes vary depending on the shoe manufacturer and there can sometimes be a difference of up to two sizes between one make and another.

You must try on the running shoe and have at least 1 cm, better 1.5 cm *room* for toe movement. You should ideally buy your shoes in the afternoon when your feet are already a little swollen and put on a thicker sock so as to be absolutely sure that there's enough room.

➤ **give your foot support. A good shoe supports and guides the foot. A bad shoe misguides your foot** as it allows your foot to shift to the left or the right on uneven surfaces or your heel to slide inwards or outwards. In any case the result is a higher amount of strain on the joints or even overstrain. The more pronounced your foot malformations are the even more important it is for the shoe to give good support.

This is the area where the most sins are committed as many runners are unaware of the foot deformities or refuse to accept that they exist in the first place. Therefore beware of very soft shoes. As well as not offering enough support there is also the danger that when there is an uneven amount of stress placed, i.e. with pes valgus, the soft layer is pressed down long-term on one side even after a few hundred kilometres. These shoes thus intensify **pes valgus** and are then extremely dangerous.

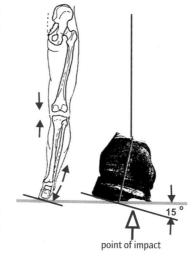

Diagram 20:
A worn-down i.e. crooked shoe-heel is like running on a slope

point of impact

15°

The weight of the shoe - contrary to many advertising slogans - hardly plays any role at all for a normal training shoe. For every 100 g of shoe weight you in turn must give 0.1% of your energy for lifting work. This means, if your well-supporting shoe is 50 g heavier than a shoe offering less support, this will cost you 0.5% more energy. However if you sink 5 mm with every step in these shoes with less support, then you must use 0.5% - 1.0%, i.e. five to ten times more energy, in order to be able to lift your body's centre of gravity again (see diagram 21). In addition to this, the wearing out of a shoe involves visko-elastic losses in the body's muscles which can bring about energy losses of up to 25%.

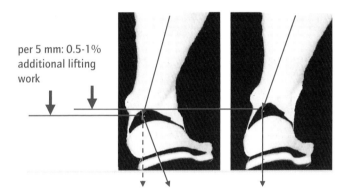

per 5 mm: 0.5-1% additional lifting work

Diagram 21:
When a running shoe is too soft and does not give enough support, the body's centre of gravity can sink down by up to 1cm. This does not only cost you extra / unnecessary energy (per 5 min: 0.5-1% additional lifting work), but implies permanent overstrain of the knee and hip joints. Over long distances these overstrains lead to premature fatigue.

▶ provide **sufficient shock absorbency**. As a rough guide the rule is: the longer the period without any physical activity and the heavier and the older the runner is, the better the shock absorbency has to be. However there is a limit to the demand for shock absorbency where there is a danger of *'sliding'* either due to territory or running speed. Similarly when malformations of the feet are very marked, the fitting and support from the running shoe are more important factors than shock absorbency.

Without good and helpful advice it is difficult to find a running shoe with the optimal amount of shock absorbency for you. A shoe which feels pleasantly 'absorbent' in the store will definitely be too soft when running. Depending on your running speed, you come down on the ground - on your shoe to be exact - with 2 - 3 times your body weight, at very high running speeds up to 5 times. The shoe must be able to cope with this load. This means when walking around the store the shoe should feel firm (not hard) on your foot.

▶ have an **intact 'unrolling' function.** The bending fold in the shoe must comply with your basic toe joints. This fold must be further to the front for runners with short toes, and further back for runners with long toes. This can be easily checked: hold the tip and the heel of the shoe between the flattened palms of your hands. Squeeze the shoe together. The bending fold must appear in exactly the same place where your toes' basic joints bend when you're running. If this isn't the case the shoe will end up affecting the joints in the front of your foot which can in turn lead to painful overstrains. For this reason be careful with shoes whose midsoles in the frontal foot area are still of equal thickness instead of becoming continually thinner, or with shoes that have pre-carved folding areas.

▶ have **soles which are slideproof and suitable for open country.** Compared with the USA only few runners in Germany run exclusively on asphalt or cement. Nevertheless a large number of shoe models are designed for this running surface at the very least through the design of the sole. For forest and field paths one normally needs well-gripping soles. One must pay attention that the treading is as V-shaped as possible and the grooves are not too narrow as otherwise stones get stuck in between. It's very important that the sole is firm enough in the frontal foot area in order to avoid the very unpleasant feeling of sharp stones cutting in.

Asphalt and cement surfaces grant the strongest grip in particular when one 'drags' one's feet, i.e. when setting down one drags one's foot a little further along the ground . The sole is thus rubbed away sooner or later.

➤ be **durable** and be a **reasonable price**. Running shoes nowadays wear longer than they used to. Nevertheless one can only expect them to be suitable for use for 1 000 - 1 500 km; 2 000 km are an exception.

The price margin is still colossal. It ranges from 25 Euro for *bargains* to 150 Euro for 'flagships' and sophisticated models. For many prices there are only several strategic but few technical reasons. What's particularly true in the case of shoes is:

"all that glitters isn't gold"!

There is such a huge offer of suitable running shoes at prices lying between 70 Euro and 100 Euro – a wide margin even for a beginner- that spending more can only be justified in exceptional cases.

Besides training shoes there are also competition models available; they are normally lighter, have less shock absorbency and because they offer less support they should only be used in competition over short distances, i.e. up to 10 000 m at the most. The shoe's supporting function is the decisive factor over long distances as already mentioned. That many runners go against the laws of physics and cover, e.g. the difficult marathon distance, wearing totally unsuitable shoes does not stem from the head but from one's personal feeling.

Finally a request to parents of young runners. Only the best shoe is good enough for a child's feet even if it costs the same as an adult's shoe.
Up to the age of 15 children's feet are formed or malformed!
Wearing proper shoes, above all shoes that are big, i.e. long enough, prevents the occurrence of malformations later. A recent widespread study showed that 50% of all children are wearing shoes which are two (!!!) sizes too small. It makes more sense to buy shoes slightly too big and wear them out completely then to buy shoes which fit perfectly and then - because they're still relatively new - to keep on wearing them when they've got too small. A shoe which is too small is the most frequent cause of a splay foot later.

7.1 Which Shoe Is Right for You?

To answer this question the following details are necessary:

➤ How high is your running speed - less than (= fast) or more than (=slow) 6 min/km?

➤ Your weight: < 65 kg (light), 65 - 80 kg (middle), > 80 kg (heavy)?

➤ How often do you train in the week - do you have a different pair of shoes for each day of training?

➤ Number of training runs over 20 km?

➤ Where do you want to wear the shoe - road, field or forest paths?

➤ Have you long or short toes?

➤ Have you foot malformations?

➤ Do you need a shoe with good pronation compensation?

➤ Experience to date with running shoes?

Unfortunately, good advice as to what running shoe is suitable for you, is an exception nowadays even in specialised stores. For this reason several specialist magazines and individual manufacturers offer an overall view on this issue where the above questions can be answered. Due to today's permanently changing models it is not possible to look at individual makes at this point.

7.2 Shoe Insoles

If changing over to a more suitable shoe still hasn't quite done the job then sticking in a special insole for splay feet may be of help if you have this problem slightly. However it must be in the right place!

If more intensive corrections are needed in the inner sole than you should get a sport insole specially made for you. These are always insoles for the entire sole (half-insoles slip!) and must be made to fit your running shoe. As well as cork and foam combinations, gridded high-pressure polythene foam has also proved to be ideal material for insoles but very few specialists insert these insoles as yet. In any case the insole must be firm enough to give support and elastic enough so as not to impair the foot's unrolling movement. Great advances in findings are expected here in the next few years.

8 Can I Lose Weight from Running?

This is a question often asked by beginners and it can be answered with **"Yes, but only if......."**.

The 'Yes' depends on a combination of the following questions:

➤ Which metabolism do you train in - in anaerobic or aerobic carbohydrate metabolism or in fat metabolism?

➤ How long are your training runs?

➤ How often do you train a week?

➤ What other energy-consuming activities do you do?

➤ What does your normal diet look like?

If you train in anaerobic metabolism as described in detail in chapter 2 it is impossible for you to lose weight as only 5% of the energy contained in carbohydrates is used and the rest is given back to the body in the form of lactic acid.

If you run in aerobic metabolism and even nearly empty your carbohydrate depots completely, it is unlikely you will lose weight without any additional dietary measures as the body fills up these carbohydrate depots again within a very short time.

It's only possible to lose weight if you trot for an hour once a week and in the process manage to reach fat metabolism. For example with a weight of 70 kg and a medium speed you use up approx. 665 kcal (about 2 750 joule), i.e. you burn off carbohydrate and fat. Running in fat metabolism is a basic requirement if you wish to lose weight through running as fat is only burned out under these conditions. - We don't want to talk about the various diets at this point.

Just how high energy consumption is with various forms of sport can be seen in the table - whether or not you have trained within fat metabolism can be determined by your lactate rate (<=2 mmol/l) or your pulse rates when running, when they have stayed well under 70%. (The areas of pulse load vary according to the type of sport.)

One can significantly lose weight when one increases training duration up to 1.5 or 2 hours. The stores of carbohydrate and fatty acids are well emptied and the 'cushions of fat' which have developed are gradually broken down. However one can only manage such long training runs with a very good state of training. For a beginner they are neither effective nor a good idea, as he either won't hold out in the first place or is in danger of overstraining his muscles.

Just as important as running in fat metabolism is the *thousand-dollar question:*

"What do you do about nutrition?"

All combinations here are not only possible but also the norm.

➤ Some people run many long distances because they love eating, and then they don't put on weight.

➤ Others wonder why they don't lose weight despite their frequent runs in the anaerobic/aerobic carbohydrate area and little food - they can't get into their heads that they're training in the wrong load area.

➤ Others again have both under control and stay nice and slim.

Running helps us to hold our weight more than any other form of sport as running is one of those forms of sport with the highest energy consumption:

body weight	sleeping	4 km/h walking	25 m/min swimming	15 km/h cycling	cross-country skiing	10 km/h running	
55 kg	55 230	151 633	242 1.013	296 1.239	495 2.072	523 2.188	kcal Joule
70 kg	70 293	193 806	308 1.290	377 1.577	630 2.638	665 2.746	kcal Joule
80 kg	80 335	225 921	352 1.474	430 1.802	720 3.014	760 3.182	kcal Joule

As well as this you don't normally eat anything 3 to 4 hours before you go running as one can't run with a full stomach as we know. Many runners aren't hungry after a run either. Should you be one of the few who are hungry after running then try and satisfy this hunger with salad, cottage cheese etc. If you have eaten normally for the remainder of that day then through your physical activity you will have used up all carbohydrates intake.

8.1 Nutrition and Running

The opinions vary here! On the one hand we have runners who only run so that they can eat a lot and often and who want to burn this off again through physical activity. On the other hand we have the 'birdseed fanatics' who don't touch anything which isn't wholemeal.

There are countless theories, books and health shops where you can spend a lot of money on this topic. A lot of the time nutrition is often worked up to such an extent that it has almost become like a *question of faith*. Anyone who has not yet converted to a particular style of nutrition is in my opinion better to stay with his normal mixed diet although he should pay attention to the following points:

➤ The proportion of carbohydrates should reach 60% as much as possible.

➤ The proportion of fats should be reduced to 30%, if possible to 25% (because of the many hidden fats this proportion is mostly too high).

➤ It's better to eat a little and often, than the other way round. The stomach gets used to smaller portions.

➤ With slow chewing the feeling of repletion appears earlier than when one eats quickly.

➤ 'Hungry', eyes, which often tempt us to take *more than necessary*, can unfortunately only be satisfied with common sense. Slow eating helps here too.

➤ The time of the day is equally important: eat food rich in content in the morning and at lunchtime, in the evening only low-calorie food. All those foods which are not burnt up in the evening are stored up by the body for *'rainy days'* - this is how the fat cushions come to being one after the other.

➤ Eat a lot of fruit and vegetables as this is food which is high in vitamins and roughage and low in calories.

8.2 Running with a Full Stomach?

Most people know that one can either run badly or not at all when one's stomach is full. A large amount of blood is required for the breakdown of foods in the stomach and intestines as well as for the further transport of the nutrients acquired there. The body can then steer these flows. The blood that is needed for digestion is not available for supplying the working muscles with oxygen (see chapter 2.7). For this reason it's necessary to have food digested first so as to be able to run well.

Furthermore, there is the danger of mechanic stress loads for the heart. These can appear in the form of reflex movements with consequences for the heart muscle's system of conduction. The result can be a collapse and in the worst case cardiac arrest.

8.3 Drinking and Running

The intake and output of fluid play a decisive role for a runner and on hot days can be a matter of life and death. During energy conversion heat is produced in the muscle which is a pleasant feeling on cold days. On warm days, however, there is no cooling from outside so the body temperature rises and the body has to adjust over to its own cooling system. We all know what this is like: the body sweats, loses water which evaporates on the skin thus removing body heat.

This release of sweat (loss of water) which can amount to 2-3 litres is only possible for a limited period of time. As well as sweat the body loses valuable mineral salts which must be filled up again as soon as possible, i.e. through mineral water, mineral water with apple juice, mineral drinks, broth, tea - sweetened or unsweetened - etc.

When buying mineral water it is important to look out for as much magnesium (Mg >100 mg/l) and calcium (Ca >250 mg/l) as possible and as little sodium as possible (Na< 50 mg/l).

An apple juice spritzer, a mix of 1/3 apple juice to 2/3 mineral water, is just as good as but significantly more reasonable than most of the highly extolled mineral drinks (assuming one uses a purely natural apple juice).

On particularly hot days it is advisable to take a prophylactic drink - 0.5 l to 1.0 l - before running. You must test for yourself what the best drinks are for you personally, still mineral water, apple spritzer, tea, mineral drinks etc. as this is not as much a question of taste but rather much more a question of what you can tolerate.

8.4 Electrolyte and Running?

A runner who does proper endurance training, i.e. one hour at 60 - 80%, once or twice a week and compensates his water loss through mineral water or an apple spritzer does not need to take in any additional electrolytes just because of endurance training.

This is not the case, however, when one has frequent and long training sessions in the summer. One must make sure here to have a sufficient intake of electrolytes. Particularly important is magnesium. Magnesium is not only our most important electrolyte, but is also involved in the correct functioning of approx. 350 processes and particularly in the control of and supply to the muscles. Muscle cramp for example, particularly when it occurs in the middle of the night after intensive endurance training, is a sign of a magnesium deficiency.

The body finds it difficult to absorb magnesium, it is therefore advisable to take only small amounts daily over a long period of time (two to three months). A rule of thumb here: when one takes twice the amount, only 20% is absorbed and the remainder is emitted from the body as *costly* urine. The only side effect I'm familiar with when too much has been taken is diarrhoea. All other side effects are on the enclosed leaflets. Magnesium is not 'doping' medicine and can be bought in all pharmacies.

You must always take care not to take magnesium and calcium together as the effects of both substances are neutralised. If you want to take both, then take one in the morning and the other in the evening.

Women in particular should get their iron levels checked regularly, not only the haemoglobin content but also iron reserves. Iron deficiency is very often the cause of an otherwise incomprehensible drop in performance.

8.5 On a Diet and Still Running?

!

Be careful!!! As regards this question I must address the women in particular as they experiment more with diets than men do. **Be particularly careful with crash diets + running** as some runners count on losing an optimal amount of weight with this measure.

This seldom works - where are you meant to get the energy to run if all energy reserves are empty from the crash diet. A car can't drive without petrol either. In LAUF-TREFF I've often experienced crash-diet runners who just weren't able to go on any longer after half an hour or even got weak and dizzy. They were quite simply totally burnt out. This is especially the case with beginners because they have very low fatty acid deposts.

Care must be taken with all diets where the body is one-sidedly withheld or even deprived of certain nutrients. Included here are those teas which are meant to drain or purify the body and other similar drinks. With these teas the body is often deprived of important minerals, e.g. potassium, calcium, magnesium etc. The combined work of these elements is still an area which we know very little about, but what we do know is that a balanced relationship between them is required for the proper working of the muscles.

9 Exercises and Other Types of Sport

Running is endurance training and exercises your cardiovascular system as well as your entire trunk and leg muscles. However endurance training is only one of five basic forms of training:

- Co-ordination training
- Flexibility training
- Speed training
- Strength training
- Endurance training

Each of these basic forms requires **individual** and specific training. They may all have an effect on each other but you cannot substitute one form with another. This means if you wish to improve your speed you must do sprint training, if you wish to improve your flexibility then gymnastic exercises are necessary.

Anyone who concentrates only on endurance training needn't wonder if his athletic fitness is one-sided, too, and he becomes as stiff as a board.

Co-ordination and speed training during one's childhood and youth are of significant importance. Foundation stones are laid here which later on life can only be learned with great difficulty or not at all. This is why these forms of training are more important at these ages than one-sided endurance training!

One needs strength, e.g. for lifting, throwing, thrusting but also for running uphill; speed strength is needed for sprinting and springing. These forms of training reach a climax from youth onwards particularly between the age of 18 and 30 and with time become less important after the age of 60.

Gymnastic exercises on the other hand are for flexibility and strength training. The shortened muscles from endurance training must be stretched again so as to stay flexible. Flexibility training is, next to or even before endurance training, the most important basic form of training and should be carried out from as young an age as possible to as high an age as possible.

With this in mind one ought to know that a muscle has only one method of working: contraction. In order for it to be stretched again a counter-muscle (anatagonists) is needed which pulls it back out. Both muscles must be in balance with each other from a strength point of view. Let me illustrate this with the example of the back and abdominal muscles.

Diagram 22:
The abdominal muscles stretch the back muscles. Both must be in balance with each other. Only regular exercises strengthen the abdominal muscles.

The back muscles as the supporting muscles are exercised with each session of running training but also through long sitting or standing. The counter-muscles to the back muscles (antagonists) are the upright and oblique abdominal muscles. These must be strengthened to such an extent that they are strong enough to completely stretch the back muscles after each (running) training session and to keep up this stretch.

If the abdominal muscles are too weak, the necessary stretching of the back muscles doesn't take place. They become continuously shorter. As well as this a hollow back begins to form which is associated with a forward tilting of the pelvis and a *flabby stomach*.

Tilting the pelvis forward implies for the runner a shortening of his stride length and thus a deterioration in his competitive performance. However, this is a minor aspect compared to the numerous problems attributed to the shortening of the back muscles, i.e. pain in the back, the intervertebral discs, the sciatic nerve and sometimes even headache. It merely shows how hard it is to get it into one's head that doing specific gymnastic exercises is more effective for achieving good competition results than the running time lost in the process.

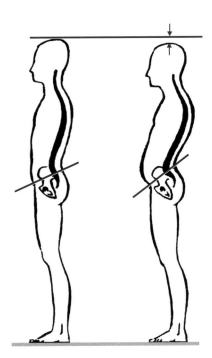

Diagram 23:
Tilting the pelvis forward changes the entire body statics and leads to a so-called hollow back. For the runner this means a shortening of his stride length and thus a deterioration in his competition results. This is not so important however compared with the countless problems which occur as a result of this shortening of the muscles: e.g. pain in the back, the intervertebral discs, the sciatic nerve and occasionally even headaches.

Just how important these exercise are for a runner has been proved in a study by the University of Tübingen the results of which show that runners who don't do any compensatory exercises are injured considerably more often and tend to have pain around the spinal area much more so than runners who train a lot and regularly do specific exercises.

Specific, we also talk these days of functional exercises which begin at the toes and finish at the cervical vertebra, **take at least one hour and** should be supervised for correction purposes. If there is nobody supervising there is a danger of one carrying out inaccurate - easier - movements which therefore don't stretch the muscle intended for stretching. One is better to go to a sports club for these supervised exercises rather than a fitness studio. In the fitness studios exercises are often carried out which one can already do and not those exercises which are badly needed.

As a supplement to all types of sport one should complete such a session of exercises at least once a week. Twice a week would be optimal. In the appendix you can find examples for stretching and strengthening the abdominal muscles - these you can do at home.

It is not physiological sound practice however to do such stretching exercises 5 to 30 minutes into an endurance training session, which is still the case in several LAUF-TREFFs. The pulse and therefore the oxygen supply drops too dramatically in this phase as we saw in diagram 8.

On the other hand if one wishes to do speed and interval training within the anaerobic/aerobic threshold then it would be advisable to carry out intensive stretching and loosening exercises after the warm-up phase.

Before running you should do stretching exercises only if you're completely able to do so. Otherwise there is a danger of you tearing or injuring your 'cold' muscles.

Swimming and cycling are not only good supplements to running, but when one is injured for example these two forms and e.g. aquajogging are a suitable alternative to running, as one's heart and circulation are being exercised just as well here. One goes easy on the joints however as they are not under the strain of one's body weight.

10 Appendix

The small selection here of exercises for stretching and strengthening the abdominal muscles is designed to encourage you to supplement your running with specific exercises.

At the beginning at least it is advisable to do these exercises under the supervision of a qualified sports teacher so as to avoid making evasive movements and to learn to tense up the posterior muscles properly, and for women the muscles of the pelvic floor as well.

Before you begin the exercises you must move around a bit for a few minutes - slow trotting on the spot is about the best.

Complete the exercises slowly and accurately and not with a jerk. Keep this tensing up for approx. 20 seconds each time. Always have the posterior muscles tensed too. Each exercise should be repeated between 5 and 20 times.

1. Stretching exercises:

1A Stand in a doorway, raise one arm up to behind the upper door frame and bring the other arm down to the front holding the outer frame. Push the upper body forward, so far that a stretched feeling occurs in the back. Tense up posterior and abdominal muscles.

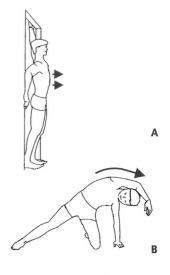

1B Stretching of the lateral back muscles, oblique abdominals and the lumbar muscles. This exercise can be done standing up as well.

1C Stretch the legs out alongside each other. Keeping the back as **straight** as possible bring the arms toward your feet thus stretching the lumbar muscles.

C

1D Your back is stretched, push your arms out on the floor in front of you, then set your posterior down on your heels. Stretching of the back and arms.

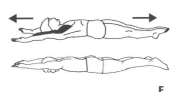

D

1E In a frog position push the back upwards, stretching it as far as the cervical vertebrae.

E

1F Stretch the arms and the legs, lie down on your back or your stomach with your legs and arms totally outstretched. Hold this tension and gradually intensify it. First of all both arms and legs together, then right arm and right leg, then the same for left, and finally diagonally.

F

1G Stretch the flexed foot up to the ceiling, straighten the knees, keep foot bent. Press the other leg-which is completely stretched as far as the toes - down onto the floor. At the same time make sure that the back doesn't lift from the floor.

G

1H Bend and pull one knee in towards the chest, stretch out the other leg and foot completely and press down on the floor.

H

1I Lay left arm down along the side of your body, the outstretched leg is relaxed. Now bend the other leg to make a right angle and let it sink down over the stretched leg towards the floor. With your right hand pull it nearer to the floor towards the chest. Press the back down onto the floor, it must not lose contact with the floor.

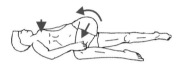

I

2. Strengthening exercises for the abdominal muscles

2A Bend the knees and hips to form right angles and outstretch the arms horizontally in front of you. The lower legs can lie on a bench or a chair. Lift the upper body slowly and push the arms in the direction of the feet.

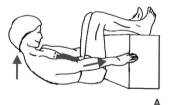

A

2B Same starting position - with arms crossed out in front of you.

B

2C Same starting position - raise the upper body, first of all lift the right shoulder up from the floor and guide the hands past the left thigh. Go back into starting position, then lift the left shoulder from the floor and lead hands past the right thigh. This is the most difficult but also the most effective exercise for the oblique abdominal muscles!

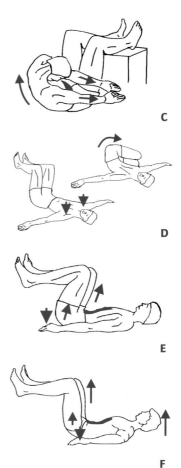

C

D

2D Same starting position - lay your hands out to the side. Legs are slightly open. Move the knees to the left and the right as far down to the floor as possible, without setting down.

E

2E Bend the knees and press the arms down firmly on the floor. Pull the thighs in toward the chest, lift the posterior and hold up for approx. 10 seconds. Lower the posterior again, unrolling each vertebra one after the other.

F

2F Form a right angle at the knees and the hips, the arms are close beside the body. Press the arms down firmly on the floor. Raise the head slightly and move the knees upwards without the thighs moving toward the chest. The posterior should also be raised from the floor. Hold this position for 10 seconds if possible.

2G Same starting position - this time with the backs of the hands on the floor.

G

Excercises 1A, 1E, 1G-1I, 2A-2G are from: "Funktionelles Bewegungstraining" Lenhart, P./W. Seibert, Sportinform-Verlag, and have been slightly modified, Excercises 1B-1D, 1F are from teaching material of the German Athletics Federation.

Photo and Illustration Credits:

Cover Photo: Polar Electro GmbH
Cover Design: Birgit Engelen
Illustrations: Claudia Jelinek

Literature

AIGNER, A. (Hrsg.): Sportmedizin in der Praxis. Springer-Verlag, Berlin (1986).

BENNER, K. U.: Atlas der Anatomie. Bertermünz Verlag Augsburg (1997).

BÖNING, D.: Muskelkater – Ursachen, Vorbeugen, Behandlung. In: Dtsch. Z. Sportmed. Sonderheft 1988, 4-7.

BÖNING, D.: Muskelkater. In: Dtsch. Z. Sportmed. 2/2000, 63-64.

DIEM, C.: Ozon – oben zu wenig, unten zu viel. In: Triathlon & Duathlon 3/1994, 53-54.

DIEM, C. J.: Der Laufschuh – das wichtigste Kleidungsstück der Läufer. In: Krankengymnastik 2/1998, 258-271.

DIEM, C. J.: Rendezvous zum Sport (20 Jahre LAUF-TREFF). In: CONDITION 10-11/94, 34-37.

DIEM, C. J.: Muskelkater – Was ist das?. In: CONDITION 3/00, 14-15.

DIEM, C. J.: Das Anfangstempo ist entscheidend. In: CONDITION 1/1985, 24-25.

DIEM, C. J./ W. SCHWEBEL: Gesundheitsförderung durch Lauftherapie – Welche Möglichkeiten bietet der LAUF-TREFF? Hilf dir selbst: Laufe. Alexander Weber (Hrsg.), 100-114, Jungfermann Verlag, Paderborn (1999).

GABRIEL, H./W. KINDERMANN: Immunsystem und körperliche Belastung: Was ist gesichert? In: Dtsch. Z. Sportmed. Sonderheft 1/1998, 93-99.

HARTMANN, S./P. BUNG/P. PLATTEN/R. ROST: Sport und Schwangerschaft. In: Dtsch. Z. Sportmed. 7-8/1997, 282-289.

HECK, H./A. MADER/R. MÜLLER/W. HOLLMANN: Laktatschwellen und Trainingsteuerun. In: Dtsch. Z. Sportmed., Sonderheft 1996, 72-78.

HECK, H./P. ROSSKOPF: Die Laktat-Leistungsdiagnostik – valider ohne Schwellenkonzepte. In: TW Sport+Medizin 5/1993, 344-352.

HESSISCHES MINISTERIUM FÜR JUGEND, FAMILIE UND GESUNDHEIT: Ozon. Referat Presse und Öffentlichkeitsarbeit Wiesbaden (1992).

HOLLMANN, W.: Lebensverlängerung durch sportliche Aktivität. In: Spektrum der Wissenschaft 10/1987, 22-28.

HOLLMANN, W./T. HETTINGER: Sportmedizin – Arbeits- und Trainingsgrundlagen. 3. Aufl. (Studienausgabe), Schattauer Verlag, Stuttgart (1990).

HOLLMANN, W.: Ozon: ein Sportkiller. In: Die Fitmacher 3/93, 5.

ISRAEL, S./J. FREIWALD/M. ENGELHARDT: Zielgerichteter Alterssport – Kraft an erster Stelle. In: TW Sport+Medizin 6/1995, 367-374.

JANSSEN, P. G.: Ausdauertraining – Trainingssteuerung über die HF- und Milchsäurebestimmung. In: Beiträge zur Sportmedizin, Bd 34, Perimed Fachbuch-Verlag, Erlangen (1989).

KLEINMANN, D.: Laufen – Sportmedizinische Grundlagen, Trainingslehre und Risikoprophylaxe. Schattauer Verlagsgesellschaft, Stuttgart (1996).

KNEBEL, K. P.: Fitnessgymnastik. rororo-Sport 8636, Reinbeck (1991).

LIESEN, H./W. HOLLMANN: Ausdauersport und Stoffwechsel – insbesondere beim älteren Menschen. Wissenschaftliche Schriftenreihe des DSB, Bd. 14, Verlag Karl Hofmann, Schondorf (1981).

MARÉES, H. de: Sportphysiologie. 8. Aufl., Sport & Buch Strauß, Köln (1996).

MARKWORTH, P.: Sportmedizin – Physiologische Grundlagen. rororo Sport 17049, Rowolth Taschenbuch Verlag, Reinbeck (1998).

NEUMANN, G.: Marathon, eine Stoffwechsel-Disziplin. In: Spiridon 7/1990, 19-22.

NEUMANN, G.: Laktatorientiertes Ausdauertraining – Grenzen erkennen, valide Möglichkeiten nutzen. In: TW Sport+Medizin 6/1993, 417-424.

NEUMANN, G.: Regeneration, welchen Wert haben Erholungsphasen für den Sportler? In: Sports Care 3/1997, 2-3.

NIGG, B.: Biomechanics of running shoes. Human Kinetics Publisher, Champain/Illinois (1986).

PESSENHOFER, H. /G. SCHWBERGER/P. SCHMID: Zur Bestimmung des individuellen aerob-anaeroben Übergangs. In: Dtsch. Z. Sportmed. 1/1981, 15-17.

PETERS, C./C. MUCHA/H. MICHNA/H. LÖTZERICH: Vergleichende Untersuchung zum Immunstatus trainierter und untrainierter Junioren und Senioren. In: Dtsch. Z. Sportmed. Sonderheft 1/1998, 111-114,

REINHARDT, L/K. G. WUSTER: Sportliche Belastung bei einer Schwangerschaft. In: Dtsch. Z. Sportmed. 46 Nr. 2, S. 132-133 (1995),

SCHLEMMER, W./M. SCHMITT: Sportmedizin und Pharmazie. Wiss. Verl.-Ges., Stuttgart (1990)

SCHMIDT, M./A. KLÜMPER: Basisgymnastik für Jedermann, Reba-Verlag, Darmstadt (1989).

SCHNACK, G.: Intensivstretching und Ausgleichsgymnastik. Deutscher Ärzte-Verlag Köln (1992).

SCHULZ, H./F. MÜLLER/A. FROMME/H. HECK: Die Belastungsintensität bei Freizeitläufern. In: Dtsch. Z. Sportmed. 7-8/1997, 270-273.

SHEPHARD, R. J./P. N. SHEK: Richtig dosiertes Training – auch im Alter eine Hilfe für das Immunsystem. In: Dtsch. Z. Sportmed. 5/1995, 283.

SIMON, G./A. BERG/H. H. DICKHUTH/A. SIMON-ALT/J. KEUL: Bestimmung der anaeroben Schwelle in Abhängigkeit vom Alter und von der Leistungsfähigkeit. In: Dtsch. Z. Sportmed. 1/1981, 7-14.

TITTEL, K: Beschreibende und funktionelle Anatomie des Menschen. 8. Aufl. (1978), VEB Fischer Verlag, Jena.

UHLENBRUCK, G./D. LAGERSTROM/P. PLATEN: Gesundheitsorientiertes Ausdauertraining. Medice – Iserlon, Echo-Verlags-GmbH, Köln (1994).

WEBER, A.: „Ich fühle mich unglaublich wohl" – Warum Läufer laufen. In: Herz & Gesundheit 4/1981, 17-19,

WILLMES, K. P.: Ozon-Diskussion – Die Panikmache ist unverantwortlich. In: Aktiv-Wirtschaftszeitung Hessen Nr. 9, 20.08.94.

WOLPERT, W./G. BECKER: Der Einfluss muskulärer Dysbalancen auf die Verletzungsanfälligkeit. In: Krankengymnastik 8/1997, 1311-1316.